STICKHANDLING THROUGH THE MARGINS
First Nations Hockey in Canada

Some of hockey's fiercest and most passionate players and fans can be found among Canada's First Nations populations, including NHL greats Jordin Tootoo, Jonathan Cheechoo, and Gino Odjick. At first glance the importance of hockey to the country's Aboriginal peoples may seem to indicate assimilation into mainstream society, but Michael A. Robidoux reveals that the game is played and understood very differently in this cultural context. Rather than capitulating to the Euro-Canadian construct of sport, First Nations hockey has become an important site for expressing rich local knowledge and culture.

With stories and observations gleaned from three years of ethnographic research, *Stickhandling through the Margins* richly illustrates how hockey is played and experienced by First Nations peoples across Canada, both in isolated reserve communities and at tournaments that bring together participants from across the country. Robidoux's vivid description transports readers into the world of First Nations hockey, revealing it to be a highly social and at times even spiritual activity ripe with hidden layers of meaning that are often surprising to the outside observer.

MICHAEL A. ROBIDOUX is an associate professor in the School of Human Kinetics and the Indigenous Health Research Group at the University of Ottawa.

MICHAEL A. ROBIDOUX

Stickhandling through the Margins

First Nations Hockey in Canada

UNIVERSITY OF TORONTO PRESS
Toronto   Buffalo   London

© University of Toronto Press 2012
Toronto   Buffalo   London
www.utppublishing.com
Printed in Canada

ISBN 978-1-4426-4523-3 (cloth)
ISBN 978-1-4426-1338-6 (paper)

Printed on acid-free, 100% post-consumer recycled paper with vegetable-based inks.

Library and Archives Canada Cataloguing in Publication

Robidoux, Michael A.
Stickhandling through the margins : First Nations hockey in Canada /
Michael A. Robidoux.

Includes bibliographical references and index.
ISBN 978-1-4426-4523-3 (bound)   ISBN 978-1-4426-1338-6 (pbk.)

1. Hockey – Social aspects – Canada.   2. Native peoples – Sports – Canada.
3. Native hockey players – Canada – Social Conditions.   I. Title.

GV848.4.C3R624 2012   796.962089'97071   C2011-908385-x

This book has been published with the help of a grant from the Canadian
Federation for the Humanities and Social Sciences, through the Aid to
Scholarly Publications Program, using funds provided by the Social Sciences
and Humanities Research Council of Canada.

University of Toronto Press acknowledges the financial assistance to its
publishing program of the Canada Council for the Arts and the Ontario Arts
Council.

University of Toronto Press acknowledges the financial support for its
publishing activities of the Government of Canada through the Canada Book
Fund.

For Sharon, Sarah, and Hannah

Contents

Acknowledgments ix

Introduction 3

1 Coloniality and the Enduring Legacy of Modernity 15

2 Healing through Hockey: Finding One's Spirit on the Ice
in the Esketemc First Nation 28

3 First Nations Hockey Tournaments: Celebrating Culture
through Sport 59

4 Constructing the Other through Hockey 110

5 Hockey as Border Thinking 130

Conclusion 145

References 153

Index 161

Acknowledgments

This book would not have been possible if not for the amazing support and guidance I have received over the past ten years researching and writing on this topic. I have to begin with Neil and Don Jones, whose initial introduction to the world of First Nations hockey was invaluable. I am so grateful to Don and his long list of teammates who welcomed me into the various hockey and social settings that made the project such an enjoyable experience. I wish to thank all the tournament organizers and tournament supporters who took time out of their busy schedules to assist me in learning about the tournaments and the levels of participation. In particular I wish to thank Harley Chingee, Sheldon Bjorklund, Margaret Kenequanash, the late Stan Indian, and the late Walter Kakeptum for all of their help throughout the fieldwork. I am especially grateful to Margaret for providing me the opportunity to volunteer at the tournament and participate in many of the social gatherings. Special thanks also to Harley for taking the time to review the manuscript and offer editorial and content comments.

I cannot say enough about how grateful I am to the people of the Esketemc First Nation and the Sandy Lake First Nation for allowing me and my students to share in their cultural practices and welcome us so warmly into their communities. While it is impossible to thank everyone individually, I wish to at least acknowledge Ken Johnson, Irene Johnson, Fred Johnson, Arthur Dick, Joseph Meekis, Norris Meekis, Donna Meekis, Russell Kakeptum, Ozzie Kakepetum, Thomas Fiddler, Fabian Crowe, Chief Adam Fiddler, Chief Dave Belleau, Council members, and Health Clinic nurses and staff. Your generosity and hospitality were truly overwhelming.

I have been fortunate to have been surrounded by many colleagues and students who supported and assisted me throughout this work, which was instrumental for the ultimate completion of this project. Thank you to Dr Pauline Greenhill, Dr Victoria Paraschak, Dr Christine Dallaire, Dr Jean Harvey, Dr François Haman, Dr Courtney Mason, Ya-Wen Lin, Michael Hirst, and David Nishizaki. Additional thanks goes to Courtney for reviewing the manuscript and providing me with insightful feedback.

A final and most special thank you to my wife, Sharon, and two daughters, Sarah and Hannah, who saw me leave on extended trips to carry out the field research for this project. I can only hope that this book can in part make up for those long absences. I thank my parents and Sharon's parents for assisting in making these trips more manageable. I am particularly indebted to my mother-in-law, Nancy Polhill, for always making herself available to fly in and stay with my family during fieldwork. Most sincere thanks to all of you.

STICKHANDLING THROUGH THE MARGINS

Introduction

As C.L.R. James used to say, Beethoven belongs as much to West Indians as he does to Germans, since his music is now part of the human heritage.
　　　　　　　　　　　　　　　　　　　– Edward Said, *Culture and Imperialism*

The connection between Trinidadian political activist C.L.R. James and the game of ice hockey (to be referred to as hockey from this point forward) as played by First Nations peoples in Canada may not be immediately obvious to readers, yet after spending four years travelling across the country studying and participating in First Nations hockey events, I could not imagine a more appropriate association. There are of course James's writings on the colonial condition (1963b, 1969), as well his classic work on the game of cricket in the West Indies (1963a), which shed some light on this relationship; but it is likely James's own personal (and perhaps unresolved) struggle for identity within the two worlds of colonial disenfranchisement and the Western European establishment that speak powerfully to First Nations peoples and the game of hockey in Canada. At one point in *Beyond a Boundary* James writes: 'I became one of those dark men whose "surest sign of . . . having arrived is the fact that he keeps company with people lighter in complexion than himself"' (1963a, 59). This notion of 'arrival' speaks to James's struggle as a revolutionary and as an individual attempting to thwart the oppression of colonialism from *within* the dominant Western European tradition, not from the overtly oppressed colonized position from which he was born (King 2001). This is a critical point for Edward Said, who writes in *Culture and Imperialism* (1993), 'narratives of emancipation and enlightenment in their strongest form were also narratives of *integration* not separation, the stories of people who had been excluded from the main group but who were now fighting for a place in it' (xxvi). In researching and writing about First Nations peoples playing and embracing the game of hockey – one of Canada's most powerful national symbols – this notion of 'integration' resonated with me throughout as I attempted to make sense of this complex and dynamic cultural phenomenon.

The complexities I am referring to here lie in the historical and political developments of hockey in Canada, Canadian identity/nationalism, and Euro-Canadian colonization of Canada's First Nations peoples. In previous works (Robidoux 2001, 2002) I have attempted to illustrate how hockey has and continues to play an instrumental role in Canadian nationalistic formulations. These works identify nation-building efforts that embody elements of eighteenth- and nineteenth-century romantic nationalism, whereby a mythologized past extensively borrowed from First Nations cultural heritage, informing Canadian national imaginings. Noticeably absent from this analysis, however, is the manner in which these nationalistic endeavours impact(ed) the very people early North American settlers colonized in order to make these imaginings possible. In other words, efforts to construct a sense of national identity through sport inversely acknowledge the potentially assimilatory effects these national sporting practices might have on marginal or minority groups.

Utilizing sport as part of imperialist conquest has been well documented by sport historians and sociologists (Gems 2006; Guttmann 1994; McDevitt 2004), whereby the playing field becomes a source of instruction for the newly colonized to assume qualities and customs of the empire. In early twentieth-century Canada, where aggressive treaty signings became the primary source of governmental control over First Nations peoples, sport complemented these strategies, effectively engaging First Nations peoples in dominant cultural practices. In other words, sports such as hockey became perfect assimilatory strategies that government and religious organizations (both often in the shape of residential schools) as well as employers could use to assist in incorporating First Nations peoples and making them productive members of mainstream society. Yet there lies a danger in tacitly accepting the outcome of these assimilatory intentions without actually studying the result of the colonized taking up the sport(s) of the colonizer. It is here again that I turn to the insightful commentary of C.L.R. James, who documents the West Indian embrace of cricket – undoubtedly the most perfect articulation of empire sport – not as a capitulation to British

dominance, but as a statement of West Indian resourcefulness, inge-
nuity, and pride. In an event that is illustrative of the discrimination
West Indian players endured at the hands of the British, James takes
this away from the situation:

> We became convinced in our own minds that St. Hill was the greatest of
> all West Indian batsmen and on English wickets this coloured man would
> infallibly put all white rivals in the shade. And they too were afraid of
> precisely the same thing, and therefore were glad to keep him out . . . We
> terribly wanted to say not only to West Indians but to all England, 'That's
> our boy.' And now we couldn't. (1963a)

The seemingly compromised position of the colonized taking up the
customs of the British Empire is resituated here as an act of defiance to
British authority, which, for James (unconsciously at first), fuelled his
passion for the sport.

It is from this manipulative embrace that I have approached writing
this book. Hockey as I experienced it in First Nations contexts was a
highly valued and at times even spiritual activity. The game in both
its localized form and professional National Hockey League (NHL) appearance held tremendous community significance. People I had come
to know over the course of this research were avid fans of all levels
of professional and elite hockey, being highly knowledgeable of league
and player developments and regular viewers of professional/elite
games either on television or in person. I would also regularly see
people of all ages displaying professional hockey memorabilia and
sportswear, and players were quick to sport the latest (and often most
expensive) hockey gear. On one occasion, while visiting a remote fly-
in reserve community in northern Ontario, I was waiting to meet the
Chief and council in the band office, admiring the beautiful artwork
and artefacts stylishly set throughout the room, when my focus was
drawn to the head of the room where there was a framed Montreal Canadiens hockey jersey set in a glass case with one of the more prominent community names displayed across the back. To me it was clear
early on that First Nations peoples have passionately embraced the
game of hockey, effectively altering traditional, more local sporting
practices. These practices, however, have not disappeared; they have
imposed themselves on the Euro-Canadian construct of hockey, making
hockey a key site of cultural enunciation, not cultural capitulation. In
this regard we can begin to examine First Nations hockey as a means of

'integration,' not in any assimilatory sense of the word, but in the emancipatory capacity that Said (1993) extracts from stories of enlightenment.

Research Genesis and Designs

At this point it would be useful to take a step back and discuss how this work originated and the manner in which the research was conducted. The idea for the project began while writing my doctoral dissertation on professional ice hockey. In researching the origins of hockey, which at least in its modern sense was developed by McGill University students in 1875 (Guay 1989), I was exposed to other key sport developments in Canada, in particular as they related to the game of lacrosse. The sport, which was both feared and revered in late nineteenth-century Canada, reflected as much about the ambivalent relationship Canada had (and to a certain extent continues to have) with Aboriginal peoples in this country as it did about Canada's relationship with sport. Certain sectors of the Canadian population took pride in the rugged and dangerous characteristics of the historical game of lacrosse, qualities similarly celebrated and contested in romanticized portrayals of First Nations peoples and their histories in this unforgiving land. In my dissertation, which became the foundation for my book *Men at Play* (2001), I barely touched on how these larger socio-political developments played out in the game of hockey, but it was enough to instil in me the desire to initiate a research program exploring the interrelationships between Canadian identity, First Nations peoples, and sport. It was my contention that First Nations hockey is a form of cultural expression that takes place within the borders of the dominant sport system. My objective was to ascertain if and how local designs and histories are manifested through hockey, despite its Euro-Canadian framework.

In 2002 I was fortunate to receive a Social Sciences and Humanities Research Council Standard Research Grant to conduct ethnographic research on First Nations hockey. Unlike the purely observational field research I had conducted on professional hockey, I proposed to participate whenever possible in the activities I was studying. In part, participating in the culture enabled a type of rapport building that exceeded that which is possible through observational research. I will speak more to this later. There was another reason I wished to engage in the activities, which was to gain a more intimate appreciation of the physical practices I would be studying. It is one thing as a qualitative researcher to describe what is being seen in the field, but to physically engage in these activities provides another level of sensory awareness that is simply not possible by merely watching what is taking place. For example, to engage in a loosely organized game of pick-up hockey on a frozen lake provided a visceral understanding of the experience. It brought to my attention the fact that the clearing on the ice was no more than three by five metres, which forced players to handle the puck in tight quarters. And because no one had equipment and nets were snow chunks and broken pieces of plywood, careful negotiation of puck, stick, and bodies was required to prevent people from getting hurt or playing the puck into deep snow where it would be difficult to retrieve. I was also made aware of how one's toes feel while skating in −20° Celsius weather, and how appreciative the youth were to have adults (my graduate student and me) take the time to play with them. None of these experiences would have been possible without actually engaging in the activities, and this came to serve as the basis for my book.

The plan to participate in cultural practices that were not part of my own cultural heritage required considerable forethought. I had not conducted research with First Nations peoples before and did not have a ready-made research partnership with any community, organization, or group of participants prior to receiving the funding. Keenly aware of the long history of exploitative and unethical research conducted *on* Aboriginal peoples, it was important to begin developing research alliances that could promote trust and positive experiences for all involved. I decided to approach someone I had played junior and varsity hockey with and who was of First Nations ancestry to discuss my intention to conduct research on First Nations hockey. I asked him advice on how to proceed with the project and what he thought might be a good approach to take. He was happy to learn of my interest in the subject and informed me that his brother Don was actively involved as a player in First Nations hockey tournaments. I immediately got in touch with Don, who expressed tremendous interest in the prospect of a researcher conducting a study on First Nations hockey. He began telling me about his involvement in tournament hockey and about the high-quality events that take place throughout Canada. Since he would be playing in most of the major tournaments that year, he proposed that I attend the events in which he would be playing. By my attending Don's tournaments, he could provide me with access to his network of friends, while also spending time with me to share his knowledge about the events, First Nations hockey, and his own experiences playing in these tournaments for over fifteen years.

The opportunity to attend First Nations hockey tournaments would provide important access to First Nations hockey, but as mentioned earlier I did not want to restrict this research to naturalistic observation. It was not possible to participate as a player in the actual hockey games since the events I attended were exclusive to Aboriginal peoples; however, I did hope to participate in organizational aspects of the events and participate in the social activities whenever possible. Again, Don played an instrumental role in providing me access to the players, both in the dressing rooms and during informal socializing that took place throughout the tournament. I seldom took advantage of the opportunity to spend time with players in the dressing room, because I did not want to intrude on the dressing room intimacy that many players cherish. I tended to restrict my interactions to after the game, when the hockey dimension was replaced by the social and more festive component of the tournament. My involvement with the players and other tournament participants and attendees typically took place during the evening hours, when people would meet at the local bar or nightclub for meals and nightly celebrations. It was during these times that I would be regaled with stories of past tournament heroics and hilarity. These social contexts were invaluable to me personally, but also as a way of establishing contacts that enabled my research to develop in unanticipated directions. Most notable was that through rapport building with each of the tournament communities, people began to invite me to their local reserves[1] to pursue my research at a more intimate, community level. Individuals quickly learned of the study I was conducting and wanted to make it clear that hockey was of great importance to their communities and that it was impossible to get an appreciation for the tournaments without witnessing hockey in the actual communities themselves. Visiting the communities allowed me to develop a participatory framework to the study, as I was invited to not only observe hockey, but also play. As a former junior and university hockey goaltender, I made arrangements beforehand to offer free goaltending clinics in each community, which were well attended and, from comments I received during and after the clinics, well received. During my stay in each community I was also invited to participate in other social

---

1 Slightly less than half of Canada's Aboriginal population resides in reserve communities, which are tracts of land owned by the state and held in trust for the use and benefit of a First Nation (band).

and cultural activities. As such, my work involved two primary components; one studying formal hockey tournaments, the other studying hockey as it was played at the local community level.

Tournament Hockey

In the first year of my research, I attended three tournaments with Don: the First Nation Winter Celebrations in Brandon, Manitoba; the North American First Nations Tournament of Champions in Kenora, Ontario; and the Prince George Lumber Kings Annual All-Native Hockey Tournament in Prince George, British Columbia. I attended one other, smaller, tournament in Williams Lake, British Columbia (the Alkali Lake Braves Tournament), without Don. Unlike the higher-profile tournaments that Don typically attended, the Alkali Lake Braves Tournament was part of a group of smaller, more community-based tournaments that offered a whole new array of meanings and experiences. I focus on these smaller tournaments in Chapter 3. For the two years that followed my initial research I decided it would be best to return to these same tournaments, with the exception of the Alkali Lake Braves Tournament. In this same period I also attended the Northern First Nations Hockey Tournament in Sioux Lookout, Ontario. My decision to focus on these tournaments in the second and third years was based in part on the fact that Don would be playing in most of them (the exception being the Northern First Nations Hockey Tournament), and my level of access to tournament events – at the arena and during social activities – was substantially increased when I was with Don. The other reason was that I only began to gain an appreciation of the event by the tournament's end (each tournament is typically three days long) and believed it would be better to gain a greater understanding of fewer events than to attend more but with limited access. Therefore, over the course of the three years of field research, I ended up studying five tournaments in three provinces. It should be noted that this decision prevented me from attending two major First Nations hockey tournaments: the Local 31 Métis Society Annual Hockey Tournament in Meadow Lake, Saskatchewan, and the North Battleford Indian and Métis Friendship Centre All-Native Hockey Tournament in North Battleford, Saskatchewan. Instead I attended each of the other tournaments twice (with the exception of the Alkali Lake Braves Tournament), which did pay dividends in terms of tournament access and my overall understanding of the events.

To explain the merits of such an approach it is first necessary to reveal the manner in which I conducted the research in each setting. My intention was to observe and participate in as many of the tournament events as possible. With the permission of tournament officials, I attended each event and observed the hockey games throughout the tournament. I also attended activities that occurred in conjunction with the event – for example, pow wows, craft sales, and other social events. In each case, I would record what was observed through video, photographs, and extensive note taking. During these observational contexts, I would interact with participants (players, coaches, and managers), fans, and tournament organizers. This interaction primarily involved informal conversational interviewing whereby I would gather various perspectives about the specific events, First Nations hockey tournaments, and First Nations hockey in general. Whenever the occasion permitted, I would also conduct formal audio-recorded interviews with players, fans, managers, and tournament organizers, seeking information similar to that sought out through informal conversations. In total, I conducted twenty-five formal audio-recorded interviews over the three year period. Interviews were transcribed and analysed through standard issue-focused analysis, meaning the interviews served to assist in my understanding of First Nations hockey. Weiss (1994) describes issue-focused analysis as concerning oneself 'with what could be learned about specific issues – or events or processes – from any and all respondents' (154). This type of interview analysis differs from a 'case-focused' approach, which focuses more on the individual respondent's experience rather than a general theme such as First Nations hockey.

Recreational Hockey

As mentioned earlier, as a result of my interactions with people during the hockey tournaments, I was invited to participate in and observe hockey as played in First Nations reserve communities. With budget and time restrictions, I ended up limiting my visits to two communities: the Esketemc First Nation in interior British Columbia and the Sandy Lake First Nation in northwestern Ontario. I made four trips to each community, the visits lasting between ten days and two weeks. In each setting, I was invited to play in recreational hockey games. In the Esketemc First Nation this involved travelling with a local community member to the closest hockey arena, a forty-minute drive away in the town of Williams Lake. In Sandy Lake, the community has its own arena and I had the opportunity to play in multiple ice sessions every night. With the help of student research assistants, I was able to record all on-ice activity through video and still images. I also made extensive field notes documenting my experiences in the dressing room before and after games, on the ice, and on the bench while waiting for my shift. Finally, I conducted informal and formal semi-structured audio-recorded interviews with community leaders, hockey fans, and players. Interviews focused on historical accounts of the sport, the changes over time, hockey in the present, and people's experiences with the sport. The majority of my time spent in the community involved informally interacting with community members, thus influencing my decision to conduct primarily informal interviews with willing participants to maintain a more natural style of questioning. With this said, I did conduct ten formal audio-taped interviews with community chiefs, band officials, one parent of a child who played hockey, one female adult player, and adult male players. In both communities hockey is predominantly a male activity; only one adult female from the Esketemc First Nation played hockey with the men.

What Lies Ahead

This book is primarily an ethnographic text in that I have attempted to construct a series of narratives that best reflect my field experiences over the past four years. These narratives have not gone unfettered by the theoretical imaginings I endlessly entertain, but I have made every attempt to foreground my field interpretations (which are highlighted in italics to demarcate immediate responses in the field) in relation to analytic commentary that I have been refining over the years it has taken to bring this book to fruition. That said, it is important to emphasize that the ethnographic method is shaped by an ongoing process of analysis, ultimately filtering what is observed, recorded, and narrated, only to be altered again by more fieldwork. This cyclical fieldwork/ analysis process, often referred to as 'recursive analysis' (LeCompte and Schensul 1999, 12) is addressed by Van Maanen (1983) when he writes: 'Various interpretive schemes need to be tried for relative fit and their ability to condense and order data. Propositions and hypotheses are typically worked up and examined while the data are still being collected' (252). How the actual product is communicated varies according to authorial intention and the intended audience of the work. In this case I have decided to emphasize ethnographic details for two reasons. First, the experiences I encountered over this period have been extensive in scope and complexity and warrant considerable attention. Second, the overall intention of this work is to speak to coloniality as it is currently manifested through specific cultural practices. The term coloniality is different from what is meant by colonialism, in that coloniality was made possible through colonialism and the enduring subjugation of modernity. How this plays out can be best appreciated through the actual experiences that I will attempt to relate in the following chapters. At no point, however, do I pretend to represent experience, but instead offer mediated readings of experience that I can only hope are subjected to the same rigorous scrutiny I have imposed upon them.

The book will be divided into five sections. Chapters 1 and 4 will focus on the theoretical framework that has filtered my gaze from the outset of the study. These theoretical underpinnings were not only important during the data collection process, but also for the manner in which I present my findings. These sections will expose readers to the epistemological potential I have inscribed on local cultural practices, in that I have sought to understand how local expressions become a means for articulating local knowledge and culture and how this knowledge and culture intersects with the larger 'colonial imaginary' (Mignolo 2000). The term imaginary here is not intended to connote the unreal, but rather ways in which cultures see the world. For Mignolo, 'the modern/colonial world is its self-description, the ways in which it described itself through the discourse of the state, intellectuals and scholars' (2000, 23). Therefore, local and dominant Western cultures are never discussed as independent entities, but always situated in tension or accord with larger Canadian/Western colonial influences. I am not suggesting that local practices are always undertaken with politicized aims, but that, as I intend to demonstrate, such practices can 'identify the tensions in the conflict between two local histories and knowledges,' and that 'local histories and knowledges . . . are forced to accommodate themselves' within a contemporary cultural context (ibid., 17). Within these conflicting imaginaries are the spaces/cracks that enable a polyphony of perspectives to be produced, exposing the colonial difference and, in kind, a type of thinking along the borders of the modern colonial imaginary.

The remaining chapters will focus on First Nations hockey. Here I will examine First Nations hockey in tension with the dominant Canadian sport system. The performance-based framework of sport has emerged within the colonial imaginary as the dominant sporting expression and has infiltrated even the most recreational and grass-roots sporting experiences. The highly structured nature of hockey co-erces athletes to the most finite levels of control. For this reason, sports such as hockey are used as disciplining devices that participants wil-fully engage in, shaping how they come to 'play.' Therefore, what were once localized, community-based hockey practices have been trans-formed into more urban commercial entertainment spectacles that dic-tate player involvement in the sport and ultimately the game itself. These same historical trends are currently manifesting in First Nations hockey, affecting the manner in which hockey in First Nations commu-nities is experienced and performed.

By drawing on works by authors from a wide range of disciplines, an attempt will be made to demonstrate how sport can be both a prescrip-tive mechanism imposing specific comportments on bodies and a site where disciplinary power breaks down. First Nations hockey enacts a type of bodily subjugation through rule and structure obligation *and* an ad hoc relationship of bodies producing inefficient and unstructured displays of sport. My experiences playing hockey in the communities exemplified the inability of bodies and objects to mesh, which under-mined any 'explicit and obligatory prescriptions' sport might offer (Foucault 1977, 153). In these contexts, it was this experience of bod-ies and objects coming together that made hockey so desirable, not the performative outcomes that this body-object complex is intended to produce in the modern colonial imaginary. For this reason First Na-tions hockey has become something other than a regimented system of controls for these communities, and subsequently a powerful tool of community expression.

In writing this book I have struggled to find a tone that is at once academically stimulating and accessible to general audiences inter-ested in indigenous peoples and issues. Since conducting this research I have received many queries from people (research participants, col-leagues, and various news media) asking when this book was finally going to be written. For many of the participants who assisted in this research, they expressed that they were eager to see a published work about their communities and cultural practices. And while I do wish this to be a celebratory piece on First Nations hockey, there are criti-cal components that I feel need to be addressed. I can only hope these critical dimensions can be appreciated in some fashion by a wide range of readers, in hope of expounding on the larger complexities of life in

First Nations communities. I recognize the gross limitations of being a Euro-Canadian academic writing about another culture, and I antici-pate subsequent critical dialogues that may ensue as a result of this work. If dialogue is generated as a result of producing this book, I will have successfully met the objective I set out in conducting this research: to locate cracks within the colonial imaginary in order to create new dialogic spaces for local knowledges and meanings to emerge.

1 Coloniality and the Enduring Legacy of Modernity

We could not, therefore, stop being what we never were and never will be.
– Anibal Quijano, *Modernity, Identity, and Utopia in Latin America*

This book endeavours to offer perspectives on First Nations cultural practices not only as they exist within local cultural frameworks, but also as they interact with the larger global forces that have influenced First Nations peoples for the past five hundred years. I say interact to emphasize the interrelatedness of local cultural practices and modern trajectories of power that have been for far too long understood as unidirectional and complete. Working from what Brazilian anthropologist Darcy Ribeiro (1968) postulated in *The Civilizational Process* – and from what subsequent world-systems, post-colonial, and subaltern scholars have since been arguing – I will be approaching First Nations hockey through the understanding that 'cultures are not developed and maintained in isolation, but in a continuous interrelation with one another' (6). Edward Said (1994) points out, 'the tendency in anthropology, history, and cultural studies in Europe and the United States is to treat the whole of world history as viewable by a kind of Western supersubject, whose historicizing and disciplinary rigor either takes away or, in the post-colonial period, restores history to people and cultures' (35). Said's point is that there has been a general failure to acknowledge the Other within the dialectics of cultural formation, as though dominated cultures are merely the product of imperial forces. Yet in recognizing this symbiotic relationship one should not lose sight of the overarching dimensions to cultural interrelatedness, which Immanuel Wallerstein

(1974a, 1974b) identifies as 'modernity' and the imposition of its imaginary around the world.

In working with First Nations peoples one must contend with the penetrating and devastating effects of colonization, which, paradoxically, were made possible by the supposedly felicitous emancipatory project called modernity. The constraints that First Nations peoples experience also serve as a point of departure for new cultural formulations to be realized: 'The dominated learned first to give new meaning and sense to alien symbols and images, and then to transform them and subvert them by including their own elements in all images, rites or expressive patterns of alien origin' (Quijano 1997, 32). To respond to the complexities of this cultural phenomenon I will be drawing extensively from world-systems, post-colonial, and subaltern theories, without necessarily adhering specifically to any of their tenets. I will be negotiating my way through these theoretical perspectives via Walter Mignolo's (2000) interpretations of this vast array of scholarship in his book *Local Histories/Global Designs*. In this work Mignolo selects kernels of theory to build his own theoretical platform, which he describes as 'border thinking.' For Mignolo, border thinking is his response to what each school of thought seeks to expose and dismantle: modernity and the coloniality of power. While modernity and coloniality cannot exist without each other, they must both be understood in order to envision how their usurpation can lead to new sites of knowledge production and legitimacy for survivors of their legacy. We now begin by considering in greater detail the possibility of border thinking within the modern colonial imaginary.

The Modern Colonial Imaginary

In an age often described as postmodern it may seem out of step to question the idea of modernity and its lasting impressions on contemporary existence. The notion of a *post*modernity, however, seems somewhat naïve considering the struggles of Canada's First Nations peoples to re-envision themselves in the twenty-first century. The prefix 'post' would suggest life after modernity; yet for First Nations peoples who have been subalternized through colonial invasion, modernity's dissolution seems overstated. While I am appreciative of the poignant critiques of modernity's factitious and fraudulent totalizing trajectories, these critiques have not resolved the violent and inferiorizing effects of modernity's grand narratives. I would state further that

Mary Louise Pratt's (2002) reading of the postmodern critique as 'putting an end to the center's self-interested and deluded understanding of modernity' is overly optimistic, as peripheral formulations of the Other continue to play out – at least concerning North America's Aboriginal populations – perpetuating a shameful and unapologetic self-centredness. It is therefore necessary to revisit modernity's role in establishing a contrived and increasingly vulnerable world order.

As a starting point, let me turn to Enrique Dussel's (1995) important opening premise in *The Invention of the Americas*. He writes:

> This history of world domination originates with modernity . . . I argue that while modernity is undoubtedly a European occurrence, it also originates in a dialectical relation with non-Europe. Modernity appears when Europe organizes the initial world-system and places itself at the center of world history over against a periphery equally constitutive of modernity. (9–10)

While there has been debate concerning the genesis of this 'world-system' formation, there is general consensus among scholars that this process began with a shift in epistemic paradigms that privileged reason as the only real basis for knowledge. Modernity's self-proclaimed supremacy over 'irrational' knowledge systems – and in turn the people who possess them – was justification and cause for a universal civilizing process that saw the systematic expansion of Occidental empires (Spanish and Portuguese initially, followed by French, British, German, Dutch, and later still, American) into regions previously unoccupied by European inhabitants. Venn and Featherstone (2006) suggest that this led the reorganization of knowledge to be 'bound up, on the one hand, with the effects of power and with the form of economy and governmentality emerging at the time' while subordinating 'alternative visions and trajectories . . . when modernity acquires the force of a project of worlding a world according to a singular vision and temporalization of history' (458).

Whether one points to Columbus's expeditions to South America or the dawn of the Enlightenment as the impetus for modernity, the expansionist vision modernity enacted rendered a coloniality of power that dramatically altered existence for the occupier and occupied in the years to come. Empire expansionism was accompanied by the propagation of European supremacy and the structuration of difference that legitimized the dominating mandate of modernity. In *The Theory of*

Communicative Action, Volume One, Jürgen Habermas (1984) speaks to the universal validity of rational thought as the essence of difference which has served to separate modern societies from those outside its imaginary. He writes:

> In archaic societies myths fulfill the unifying function of worldviews in an exemplary way – they permeate life practices . . . they present the sharpest contrast to the understanding of the world dominant in modern societies. Mythical worldviews are far from making possible rational orientations of action in our sense. With respect to the conditions for a rational conduct of life in this sense, they present an antithesis to the modern understanding of the world. (44)

The resulting classification of non-Western inhabitants as inferior led to, first, the philosophical justification for European domination and occupation of non-Western peoples and lands, and, second, the sub-alternization of indigenous knowledges and power structures that did not fit within this genealogical formation. Modernity is based as much on its own self-aggrandizement as it is on its projected inferior-ized subject whose Otherness confirms Eurocentric claims of universal superiority.

To take this one step further, the modern colonial imaginary endures as long as the relationship with the inferior Other, against whom modern advancements are measured, is maintained. Critical to this arrangement is the notion of progress (typically understood in Western terms, e.g., the alphabet and technology) and the seemingly advanced state of Western societies in comparison to their conquered populations. Native American scholar Vine Deloria (1978) plays with this Eurocentric envisioning of Western advancements when he writes, 'we perhaps could have been more insistent on making the non-Indians provide more and better arguments for their vision . . . Any group that frantically dug gold in the West in order to transplant it to the east and bury it cannot be quite right and their insights cannot form the highest achievement of our species' (11). Exposing the delusional vision of modern progress is likely even more profound when one considers the definitive indicator of cultural progress: technology. Modernity's vision of technology has enabled massive human and environmental destruction, unprecedented divisions of wealth and poverty, and unparalleled religious and ethnic conflict across the globe; yet modernity's faith in technology does not waver. As George Grant (1986) eloquently argues, this modernist predicament has simply created a greater dependency on technology 'to meet the emergencies which technology has produced' (16).

Modernity's particular standards of human progress would be difficult for any non-modern society to match. Progress is constructed as an evolutionary process in which modern societies have been self-identified as the convenient frontrunners. The rest of the world has simply to catch up. Pratt (2002) refers to this evaluative construct as 'time lag,' which situates non-Western peoples as 'behind and will in time catch up, so that at a particular point in the future, all will be fully and equally modern' (31). This 'point in the future' is purposively vague, maintaining the elusiveness of an eventual modern coming of age, and thus denies knowledge production from outside of modernity's epistemic. Thus, if supremacy is based in reason, those outside of this epistemological framework will forever remain outside of modernity's imaginary and maintain the coloniality of power. Until this teleological framework is subverted, modernity's consciousness will remain intact.

The challenge then is to begin locating cracks within this imaginary in the hope of giving way to alternative epistemologies and new sites of knowledge production. This should not be mistaken as an effort to somehow locate what Habermas describes as signs of 'rationality' (1984, 66) in peripheral cultures, but instead leads us to focus on ways of knowing as they intersect with hegemonic knowledge systems. The task, as Michel Foucault suggests, involves bringing to attention 'local, discontinuous, disqualified, illegitimate knowledges against the claims of a unitary body of theory which would filter, hierarchise and order them in the name of some true knowledge and some arbitrary idea of what constitutes a science and its objects' (Martin 1988, 83). In this book I will be examining how local cultural practices are expressed and negotiated within the larger matrix of coloniality. Cultural practices will be examined as 'social-semiotic interactions' to acknowledge the indeterminate levels or sites of knowledge production as manifested in everyday experience, or in other words, at the level of signs (Mignolo 2000, 14). I concur with Homi Bhabha (1991) in his recognition of the transformative potential of local cultures 'redefining the signifying relation' of signs within the present condition of modernity. Instead of searching for new or unique cultural expressions, the focus will be on local cultures reinscribing meaning on existing signs through their daily performances. At the level of sign, even the most mundane cultural expression is understood to be charged with meaning. Through their performativity within a local framework, the colonial difference is exposed without slipping into a pointless search for authenticity – questing for signs of authentic cultural practices versus those influenced or based in modernity. Expanding our scope to signs expressed and transformed through everyday life points to a type of border thinking, which leads us finally to the critical juncture of the decolonization of knowledge.

First Nations Hockey as Border Thinking

The importance of destabilizing signifying relations within the modern colonial imaginary is that it disrupts modernity's singular vision of knowledge, which has been instrumental to its formation and enduring legacy. As signs are transformed, knowledge becomes discontinuous, fragmented, and no longer locatable within modern epistemologies. The notion of 'border thinking' provides important insight into this process of alternative knowledge formation and the construction of local identities in a global environment, where the local is often constructed through the tools provided by dominant culture. To illustrate this, it is useful to consider Walter Mignolo's notion of border gnosis further, which he derives from Valentin Mudimbe's (1988) work on African knowledge systems.

Mudimbe, in setting out to explore African philosophy, discovered that his research was being guided by exoteric epistemological categories vis-à-vis Western philosophical traditions. He decided he needed to 'speak of African *gnosis*,' from the ancient Greek, meaning 'to know' (ibid., ix). For Mudimbe, gnosis captured a wider range of knowledge that '"philosophy" and "epistemology" contributed to cast away' (Mignolo 2000, 10), enabling him to approach the complexity of knowledge produced at the intersections of coloniality and traditional knowledge systems. Walter Mignolo, working from Mudimbe's notion of gnosis, introduces the notion of 'border gnosis,' which he defines as 'knowledge from a subaltern perspective . . . knowledge conceived from the exterior borders of the modern/colonial world system' (ibid., 11). Border gnoseology then, is 'a critical reflection on knowledge production from both the interior borders of the modern/colonial world system . . . and its exterior borders' (ibid.). He discusses this more effectively through the poetic process as shared by Barbadian poet Edward Kamau Brathwaite. Mignolo explains that in order to capture the rhythms and sounds of the Caribbean, Brathwaite needed to move beyond the literary traditions made known to him in colonial schools. He learned to adopt a sound of his own that was reminiscent of stones skipping over the water, yet communicated these sounds within the poetic tradition in which he was trained. Mignolo writes:

> If Brathwaite found a voice and a form of knowledge at the intersections of the classical models he learned in a colonial school with his life experience in the Caribbean and consciousness of African people's history, his poetry is less a discourse of resistance than a discourse claiming its centrality. (1993, 130)

Writing from the margins does not necessarily mean writing in opposition to dominant discourse. If anything, artists such as Brathwaite are constructing and theorizing 'about alternative centers of enunciation in what have been considered the margins of colonial empires' (ibid.).

Similarly, and more specific to the Canadian First Nations contexts in which I am working, Scott B. Vickers illustrates how recent Native American artists have 'begun to use non-traditional forms to portray Indian themes in new and idiosyncratic ways' (Vickers 1998, 111). He describes how one artist applied the 'new art ideal of cubism' to 'Indian subjects in a way that conjoined the new ideal with the long-standing tradition of Plains hide paintings and the ledger book drawing of Indian prisoners at Fort Marion, Florida' (ibid.). In Foucauldian terms these alternative discourses further fragment or decentralize knowledge, but do not necessarily run in direct opposition to it. It is more effective to assume the position articulated by Kajasa Ekhom-Friedman and Jonathan Friedman. They state that the 'local is encompassed and constituted within the global,' but is not 'a mere product of external forces. On the contrary, we have insisted on the articulation between the local and global as central to the generation of specific and social realities' (1995, 134). Therefore it is not always advantageous to question when a group is acting in resistance to dominant cultural forms or succumbing to global forces. It would seem more beneficial to consider discourse and knowledge as 'positioned practices,' which implies a fluidity between 'assimilation, encompassment and integration' of global processes (ibid., 136). By thus moving beyond this dichotomous relationship of dominance and resistance we do not reduce human experience to an endless struggle against global designs. Instead we are able to take into account what Norman Long rightfully describes as a 'complex drama about human needs, desires, organising practices, power relations, skills and knowledge, authoritative discourses and institutions, and the clash of different ways of attempting to order and transform the world' (2000, 189).

How groups construct meanings within the modern colonial imaginary has been considered predominantly through forms of artistic expression in former colonies (e.g., literature and visual art). Edward Said, Fawzia Afzal-Khan, and Padmini Mongia are examples of seminal figures who have contributed to our understanding of the complexities of cultural formation and identity within the borders or cracks of dominant Western epistemology. The expression of other cultural practices, however, also informs us of border gnosis and the manner in which cultural meanings and identities are constructed. Sport, for example, is such an important part of local popular cultures and histories that it becomes a critical site in which to observe how local designs are displayed and contested through the very forms that were imposed by colonial regimes. However, scholars have only recently paid any real attention to sport, largely because it has been understood as frivolous in nature, and not something worthy of intellectual consideration. The sharp rise in commercial profits associated with sport in the latter half of the twentieth century prompted increased interest from a variety of sectors. By the 1970s, for example, the Olympic Games were no longer the gentlemanly pursuits of aristocratic Europe; they had become high performance mega-events that held tremendous political and economic potential (Preuss 2004). The development of professional sport throughout much of the Western Hemisphere similarly evolved from individual business enterprises to massive corporate entities that signalled new opportunities for economic growth and expansion in the sport and entertainment industries. But as Richard Gruneau (1993) astutely points out, the dramatic growth of the contemporary sport industry was in itself not enough to prompt the sudden proliferation of critical sport scholarship.

Gruneau argues that it was the paradoxical appearance of sport as, on the one hand, diversionary and somewhat outside of serious social realities, and, on the other hand, an integral part of the social and cultural fabric that made it not only worthy of intellectual attention, but a fascinating area of study. For Gruneau, it was these paradoxical complexities that challenged scholars 'to integrate the analysis of the paradoxical features of sport into a broader understanding of human agency and cultural production and their expression in patterns of development, social reproduction and social transformation' (xxx). Suddenly sport was being examined as not merely a reflection of society, but rather an integral part of social and cultural formation. Scholars such as Eric Dunning (1971), Allan Guttmann (1978), Jenifer Hargreaves (1982), and John Hargreaves (1986) are among the many trailblazers in critical sport studies that offered new modes of analysing sport as cultural practice. Intersections between sport, power, class, and gender became prominent themes in sport studies scholarship, but by the late 1980s scholars such as Susan Birrell (1989) were pointing out that 'notably absent from all these critical positions, in sport studies and in the parent disciplines or fields as well, is any sophisticated, critical analysis of racial relations' (213). The lack of scholarship focusing on sport and race is puzzling considering the profound racial tensions that have surrounded sport throughout history. The formal exclusion of racial groups from organized sport, the profound insecurities of interracial sporting competitions, and deluded projections of racial superiority/inferiority through athletic prowess are issues of race that have been at the forefront of all levels of sport. Over the past twenty years, however, there has been a surge of scholarship focusing on these issues and others, and through new forms of critical race theory, issues of race and sport are being exposed.

Two prominent themes within this vast body of research are racial discrimination/oppression, and resistance. Earlier scholarship tended to emphasize the former, dismantling naïve readings of sport as the great equalizer, an even playing field where performance is based on merit, not skin colour. As research in this field grew in complexity, scholars began unravelling how within this highly prejudicial and unjust environment, expressions of resistance and cultural affirmation were possible. Scholars pointed to the work of C.L.R. James in exposing how sport has and continues to be a critical site of resistance, in this case to the colonizing forces that initially introduced cricket as a means to achieve social and cultural conformity (Carrington 1998). This theme of resistance has grown increasingly popular within American critical race research (Hartmann 2000, 230), but resonates also with scholars who have focused more specifically on indigenous experiences in the world of sport. In part this research has helped identify the proud sporting traditions of local indigenous populations from both historical and contemporary perspectives (Fisher 2002; Heine 2006; Oxendine 1988; Tatz 1995), but it also explores issues of discrimination, segregation, and resistance to racist and exclusionary practices (Diaz 2010; Forsyth and Wamsley 2006; Hallinan and Judd 2009; Hokowhitu 2009; Judd and Hallinan 2007; Paraschak 1995, 1998; Tatz and Adair 2009). These and

other scholars are inspired by the fact that 'sports have played a significant role in the colonizing and empire building processes,' but 'the
dominance of these social forces notwithstanding, sports and other
cultural practices also marked the resistance of colonized peoples who
searched for grounded social values and meanings at times when their
immediate cultural surroundings were changing' (Forsyth and Wamsley 2006, 295). Sport is regularly taken up as an important site for cultural contestation, often reproducing or resisting dominant Western
values and ideologies (Paraschak 1997). While it is not my intention
here to wade through this diverse and rich body of literature, it is important to highlight how the notion of resistance has been taken up, and
briefly address how the work at hand builds from these discussions, yet
offers an important point of departure.

In a now-classic article by Victoria Paraschak (1995) tracing Canadian federal government policy development around Aboriginal sport
in Canada from 1972 to 1981, she reveals the incongruence between the
dominant Euro-Canadian vision of sport and that of Aboriginal peoples
across the country. During the 1970s, the seemingly innocuous proposition by the federal government to fund Aboriginal sport in Canada
was rife with assimilatory initiatives, and had less to do with funding Aboriginal sport, and more to do with transforming local sporting
practices to fit into the mainstream Western system. Paraschak points
out how 'Native people at this meeting stressed that their view of sport
differed from that of the mainstream, and was informed by broader Native concerns' (7). Federal officials mistook the Aboriginal interest and
passion for sport (both of the Euro-Canadian convention and local) as
an overlapping of Euro-Canadian and Aboriginal cultures. In much of
Paraschak's work she has documented Aboriginal resistance to a Euro-
Canadian sport system and has advocated for the constant struggle to
maintain indigenous sport identities.

Paraschak's work has influenced others to pursue this notion of Aboriginal sport sovereignty as seen in Forsyth and Wamsley's (2006)
work on the North American Indigenous Games (NAIG). In this article
Forsyth and Wamsley point out that despite the Eurocentric sporting
events that make up much of the games, 'NAIG inverted centuries-old
coercive and incorporative relationships to create opportunities for Native Canadians to celebrate their cultural identities through mainstream
sport' (295). The authors argue that the Games 'came to provide a path-
way for resistance against pressures to conform to Euro-Canadian culture' (296). Forsyth and Heine (2008) pursue this argument from another

angle in their analysis of the City of Winnipeg's efforts to ameliorate their sport and recreation infrastructure and services for disadvantaged citizens. Once again we see government officials attempting to incorporate Aboriginal youth into recreation programming but without attempting to ascertain 'what Aboriginal people themselves understand to be meaningful recreation activities' (104). The article focuses not on acts of resistance to city recreation programming, but rather on the inadequacies of city programming to accommodate what Aboriginal youth deem to be meaningful recreation activities. They conclude that it is imperative that government officials 'open up alternative spaces for envisioning more inclusive opportunities for Aboriginal youth in the growing structure of sport and recreation in urban areas' (113). The emphasis is on first acknowledging the disparate recreation or sporting interests of Aboriginal peoples and subsequently locating ways that best serve these interests. According to Paraschak (1997), if activities and programs 'are not altered from their eurocanadian [sic] form' it will increase 'the likelihood that imbued eurocanadian values will likewise be reproduced by the athletes' (7).

Other scholars examining indigenous peoples engaged in mainstream activities in mainstream institutions have taken up issues of resistance differently. In *The American Indian Integration of Baseball*, Powers-Beck (2004) provides an informative account of the introduction to and adoption of the game of baseball by Native Americans. Early in the work Powers-Beck acknowledges the imperialist agenda of introducing sport in colonial contexts, pointing out that sport can be seen as both placating and distracting those groups who have been dominated by colonial regimes. But in viewing sport as such, one neglects to acknowledge how Native Americans also 'appropriate and refashion European games into their own athletic culture' (15). By playing mainstream sport Native Americans consciously accept or reject qualities of the sport to make it their own. John Bloom (2000) tackles similar issues in his work on sport in Native American residential schools. Around the world colonial governments utilized residential schools as a stern and in some cases abusive means of assimilating indigenous populations into mainstream culture. Sport was a popular tool in this regard because of its highly structured and disciplining framework. Bloom exposes the complexities around the troubling history of First Nations boarding schools that defy singular readings and interpretation, stating that 'even though mainstream sports were intended to assimilate the native children and teenagers who attended boarding schools, former students expressed a type of ethnic pride in their memories of sports, a pride that conveyed antiassimilationist sentiments' (ibid., xix). For Bloom, sport is 'far too complex and too interesting to be tied to any single set of stories' (ibid., 127). His work signals a departure from other resistance literature, which often situates behaviour as either accommodative or resistive. Donald Fisher (2002) captures this best in his work on the Aboriginal sport of lacrosse by asking: 'So what are we? Are we traditionalists or are we assimilated? If you can get away from your categories and.definitions, you will perceive us as a living and continuing society' (311). Despite global or colonial forces that inform or at times shape these sporting practices, their meanings are not predetermined by global or colonial designs; human behaviour and development is complex, thus requiring more rigorous readings of local cultural expressions and their intersections with larger global forces.

For this reason, First Nations hockey is an especially complex site whereby local and global meanings are consistently negotiated and transformed. Certainly hockey is part of the Canadian national imaginary (Robidoux 2004), yet it is similarly claimed by First Nations peoples as emblematic of their culture and identity. Adding to the complexity is the fact that the most ardent First Nations hockey fans are typically the most ardent National Hockey League fans, whose allegiance lies primarily with Canadian NHL teams. The seemingly incongruous relationship of the colonized supporting the colonizer through modern high capitalist sport entertainment on one level confirms that First Nations hockey is not constructed in opposition to Canadian/mainstream professional hockey, but rather feeds off it. In this case, sport can indeed be transformed into culturally meaningful practices that are reflective of local designs.

In this regard First Nations hockey is the embodiment of what Mignolo (2000) refers to as 'colonial semiosis,' which identifies 'moments of tension in the conflict between two local histories and knowledges,' where 'the movement forward of a global design that intended to impose itself' clashes with 'those local histories and knowledges that are forced to accommodate themselves to such new realities' (17). These tensions mark the rupture of signifying relations despite the general appearance of the stability of signs. That is to say, hockey is reproduced in both First Nations and Euro-Canadian contexts but the colonial difference ensures that systems of meanings are never intact. As First Nations peoples take up the game of hockey, whether in high performance contexts or in local vernacular settings, it is important to emphasize that this process of engagement is not necessarily an oppositional stance, but rather a disruptive one. The disruption gives way to a type of border gnosis woven within the fabric of the modern colonial imaginary. This kind of manipulative embrace exposes the importance of border thinking 'in all its complexity,' which is a means of 'thinking that emerges as a response to the conditions of everyday life created by economic globalization and the new faces of the colonial difference (ibid., 304). It is critical to move beyond notions of resistance or accommodation and begin articulating how First Nations expressions of hockey destabilize existing knowledge systems shaped by modernity.

Conclusion

In the remaining chapters, I will provide ethnographic accounts of First Nations hockey to reveal how border thinking is enabled through local cultural practices. These accounts show how First Nations cultures adapt modern Western designs to serve community needs and values. I turn first to expressions of First Nations hockey in remote local settings where community members struggle to partake in dominant sporting practices. With limited access to facilities, sporting equipment, standardized coaching, and league systems, the communities described in this study seek Western sport influence as a means of ameliorating their own sporting practices. These community efforts again demonstrate local knowledge systems in tension with global sporting practices and the colonial legacy. This will be followed by accounts of First Nations tournament settings where it will be evident how modern Western sporting frameworks and philosophies are simultaneously endorsed and subverted in First Nations performative settings. By focusing on the overarching pressures of modern Western influence on local sporting practices, it is possible to visualize the cracks within the modern imaginary that provide spaces for First Nations knowledges and meanings to be articulated. Throughout all of these examples, we will examine how the uniform Western epistemological framework of sport is fragmented through local participation, offering alternative modes of knowledge production that thwart modernity's teleological framework and lead to a vision for the decolonization of knowledge.

2 Healing through Hockey: Finding One's Spirit on the Ice in the Esketemc First Nation

Sport is, I call it the esteem of First Nations Spirit. It's just the spirit explaining itself, you know, of a life. You know, whether it's hockey, say it's hockey, I reckon my spirit is in it – it's got to expand its energy somewhere you know.
– Former Chief of the Esketemc First Nation
(personal interview)

In central British Columbia, there is a First Nations community that has gained international recognition for its battle with alcohol abuse. The population of Esketemc, a Secwepmc (typically referred to as Shuswap in English). Nation located in Esket (Alkali Lake is the English name) – pejoratively known as Alcohol Lake – at one point in the 1970s had close to a 100 per cent rate of alcohol abuse. Now the community is over 90 per cent sober (Saggers and Gray 1998; York 1989). The incredible turnaround is both an inspirational and cautionary tale, as the suffering endured has left an everlasting impression on community members. In *The Dispossessed*, Geoffrey York writes:

Since the 1940s, Alkali Lake has endured a nightmare of alcoholism and brutal violence. Now it is a symbol of hope. The people of Alkali Lake achieved sobriety, and they have become the inspiration for hundreds of other Indian communities across Canada. But the shadows of the past are never far away. This is a village where the laughter of a child is soon followed by the tears of a man or a woman. In the evening, at counseling sessions and support groups, they cry openly as memories of the past come flooding back. (176)

In December 2002 I was invited to spend time in Esket. I was invited by John,[1] a member of the community, to learn about a new hockey initiative that he had established. It was explained that this First Nations hockey initiative was designed to reflect the values and culture of the people, and was instrumental in the healing of the community. This chapter provides an ethnographic account of my experiences participating in the hockey program and the cultural practices that surround hockey, which, as was repeatedly explained to me, are all part of a long healing process. Prior to presenting these accounts, it is first necessary to reveal the acute suffering this community endured in order to appreciate the tremendous path to recovery on which community members daily embark.

The Esketemc Story

The Esketemc story, or the story of Alkali Lake, is perhaps one of the most often told accounts of a contemporary First Nations community. As Bopp et al. (1998) cautiously point out, 'the story of what happened (and is still happening) within Alkali Lake is not our story to tell . . . there is no one story. There are, rather, hundreds of stories that are blended together to make up what we will generally refer to as the "community's story."' In 1985 members of the community produced a remarkable film entitled *The Honour of All: The Story of Alkali Lake*, which documented the community's history of alcohol abuse and its path to sobriety. The film is riveting not only because of the harrowing narrative, but because the actors in the film are local community members playing themselves in the retelling of the story. The film conveys a haunting reality. In the epilogue, the actors openly express the tremendous emotions they experienced playing themselves in front of the camera and having to relive their experiences of alcohol abuse and the subsequent horrors the community endured as result of alcoholism. What I am providing here is a surface reflection of this powerful community narrative, simply to provide context about current cultural practices. The impact of these events on the community is profound. The historical details provided here build in part off of the

---

1 Where only first names are provided, a pseudonym has been used to ensure participant anonymity.

documentary, but rely also on scholarly accounts (Furniss 1987; Palmer 2005; Teit 1909; Whitehead 1981) of this region to provide broader context into the issues of alcoholism, abuse, colonialism, and struggles for healing.

The Esketemc First Nation is located in the interior central region of British Columbia, fifty-one kilometres south of Williams Lake. The community is part of a larger grouping of nineteen communities registered under the Esketemc First Nation title. Unlike most First Nations in Canada, Esketemc communities have not signed treaties with the federal government and are still in the process of establishing land claim settlements. Esket, or Alkali Lake 1, as identified by Indian and Northern Affairs Canada, is a relatively small reserve with approximately 455 residents, about fifty of whom live off-reserve or on other reserves. The community has a primary school, health centre, band office, community store, hotel, and recreational areas including an outdoor rink and rodeo grounds. The community has modern housing with contemporary Western amenities, including running water, electricity, satellite television, and internet access. The community is relatively remote despite the close proximity to the larger centre of Williams Lake. The road, which is only partially paved from the section closer to Williams Lake, winds its way through hilly terrain and, in the winter months especially, is treacherous. Despite this, many Esketemc residents rely heavily on services in Williams Lake, ranging from shopping to sport and recreation.

First Nations peoples in this region have undergone drastic lifestyle transformations. As late as the 1850s, Shuswap peoples relied almost entirely on the land for subsistence. Initial contact with Europeans occurred in the early 1800s but it was not until the latter half of the century that there was a substantial European presence. It began with the expansion of the fur trade into the region, followed by an intense yet short-lived gold prospecting boom, after which permanent Euro-Canadian settlements were established (Furniss 1987). Their encroachment on traditional territories put unprecedented strain on the local environment, depleting natural resources that were necessary for land-based subsistence. With the absence of large game like elk and moose, food and material resources (such as those for clothing and nomadic dwelling construction) were depleted. This initiated a change in Shuswap semi-nomadic lifestyles, which could not be sustained without access to sufficient natural resources, and thus created greater reliance among the Shuswap on foreign Euro-Canadian goods and technologies.

Along with permanent settlements in the region came Christian missionaries throughout the latter half of the nineteenth century. Miller (2000) has argued that likely the greatest impetus for cultural change among First Nations across Canada was not government or industry, but rather the implementation of Christian-based authority. There is no clearer illustration of this than in Esketemc lands – initially in the 1870s, and to a greater extent in the 1890s – when the Roman Catholic Church successfully implemented the 'Durieu System.' Elizabeth Furniss explains: 'Developed in 1850 by Paul Durieu, O.M.I, missionary to Oregon, this system was aimed at replacing traditional organization of the winter settlements with a system of hierarchical village organization based on Catholic beliefs and values' (115–16). Margaret Whitehead (1981) elaborates on the strict adherences demanded of the people under the Durieu system:

A bell awoke everyone at 5:00 a.m. Morning prayers began at six and were followed by a few minutes of silent contemplation, a hymn, and Mass. After breakfast a 'grand session' was held. In these sessions several matters were attended to: 'abuses' were corrected; 'delinquents' were censured; differences between individual Indians were 'terminated'; the catechism was explained, and the Indians practices new hymns. In the late afternoon, prayers and hymns were followed by benediction and a second 'grand session.' To ensure that everyone attended the services . . . Bishop Durieu posted watchmen equipped with notebooks and pencils to watch for those who succumbed to temptation. (95)

Whitehead points to the natural synchronizations of traditional Shuswap beliefs and those proselytized by the new wave of Christian missionaries (ibid., 29–32), which made the First Nations in this region more open to their presence. The 'openness' of the Esketemc people to the church must be understood critically, however, and within a context of natural resource depletion, food insecurity, and rapid lifestyle transition. Voluntarily handing over all aspects of tribal and individual authority to the church, or to any other institution, speaks to the radical changes imposed upon people in the region, but also the paternalistic stance employed in early First Nation/Euro-Canadian relations. First Nations groups had been led to expect relief from chronic upheaval, food shortages, and poverty. The Christian rhetoric of 'shepherding' was perfectly aligned with emerging colonial policies of stewardship, officially formulated in 1876 with the Canadian Indian

Act. First Nations consent to domination was manufactured by promising the people protections from the plight they now faced as a result of a Euro-Canadian presence. As wards of the state, the government and/or Christian missions were responsible for the well-being of the new 'flock,' which was difficult to resist for people undergoing such tremendous cultural, social, and economic change. Interestingly this construct of stewardship (governmental and religious) was developed from the idea that First Nations needed as much protection from external forces as they did from themselves (Miller 2000). Again the church played an important role, offering First Nations peoples salvation from their 'hedonistic' and 'savage' lifestyles, but also protection from the evils of Western influence, most notably alcohol.

In the film *The Honour of All*, it is stated that alcohol was not an issue for the community until after the Second World War, yet other historical accounts point to the early fur trade and gold rush in the mid to late 1800s as a critical point where alcohol was introduced. Government regulations prohibiting the sale of alcohol to First Nations peoples, along with the intermittent enforcement of the Durieu system, likely did limit alcohol use, but the presence of alcohol was having an impact. Furniss (1987) states that the gold rush in the 1850s brought with it opportunities 'for wage-labour employment in packing and guiding, and the availability of alcohol through the numerous saloons and roadhouses that lined the Cariboo Trail,' which 'contributed to increasingly frequent Indian use of alcohol and to drunkenness' (115). The problems of alcohol abuse escalated with changes to the Indian Act, which no longer made the sale of alcohol to First Nations people illegal, but also with the intensification of social and economic relations with Euro-Canadians. In the opening scene of *The Honour of All*, two men from the Esketemc First Nation in the 1940s are negotiating the sale of their hides at a fur trading post. The two men are trying to demand fair prices but are eventually swindled by the Caucasian clerk who plies them with alcohol. The two men are next seen leaving the premise completely inebriated and with nothing to show for their efforts. The episode reflects the broader history of Euro-Canadian influence, exploitation, and the consequent damage to local populations. For the Esketemc people specifically, the damage spiraled out of control, to the point that by the late 1960s the entire community succumbed to alcoholism.

It is here that 'the story of Alkali Lake' often starts, with the darkest days of 100 per cent alcohol abuse, followed by the step-by-step stages of recovery. Here it is necessary to focus on four key elements of this story in order to proceed with any contemporary analysis. The first is that the recovery movement was initiated from within the community. Support through a Christian Brother and Alcoholics Anonymous played an important role in the recovery process, but the instigation for change came from within the community. Second, the community's remarkable turnaround generated international recognition and eventually became an inspirational tale of sobriety and First Nations success. This story, however, is merely a snapshot in the community's history, and as Bopp et al. (1998) explain, it fails to acknowledge the ongoing suffering and struggles for healing the community continues to face:

> The story of Alkali Lake is not a fairy tale in which everybody lived happily ever after. There was indeed a dramatic turnabout in alcohol consumption. But ten years after the movie was made, Alkali Lake people are still struggling with underlying issues. While the use of alcohol was overcome in one generation of people, many of their children are now engaged in struggles of their own. The healing process is far from over.

The third element stems from the second, in that in coming to terms with alcoholism, the community was awakened to other forms of abuse they had endured in the past and which continue to haunt them today. The residential school system robbed children of their childhoods; debased cultural practices; ruptured traditional familial relations; and in some cases subjected community members to various degrees of physical, sexual, and mental abuse. There was also rampant sexual abuse within the community, which was in part triggered by the abuse people faced in the residential schools, and likely both contributed to, and was made possible through, alcohol abuse (Fournier and Crey 1997). The final element that requires attention is the fact that the Alkali Lake story is now more than twenty years old, and members of the next generation face their own struggles of abuse and addiction, which continue to put pressure on a community internationally renowned for recovery and success. Through no fault of its own, the community is pressured into living up to a model of healing that it has inspired, yet has been unable to fulfil. It is in this context that I arrived in the community to learn about a hockey program, but came away with so much more. It is here that I hope to contribute to the 'hundreds of stories' of the Esketemc First Nation, to share in its healing journey.

Hockey Reform

My reason for visiting and spending time in the Esketemc First Nation originally had nothing to do with its history or its acclaimed sobriety movement. In fact I knew nothing about the community prior to going. Instead, I received a call from an individual who had learned from a local media source that I received national funding to study First Nations hockey. John called me at my office to invite me to his community to learn about a hockey initiative he had started. He informed me that his program was designed to teach kids hockey, but in a manner that was in line with First Nations culture and spirituality. He explained that hockey was guided by the four dimensions of the medicine wheel, and that through hockey, kids were given the opportunity to develop physically, spiritually, emotionally, and mentally. His program sounded fascinating and I was keen to learn more about it as my proposed research sought to explore avenues for local cultural designs within the Euro-Canadian construct of hockey. I was excited by the opportunity to visit his community and proposed to offer a free hockey clinic for the youth while I was there. As a former goaltender, I figured I could offer a clinic specifically designed for goalies or aspiring goalies in the region. John was very receptive to the idea of the hockey clinic and offered to advertise it to the community and arrange for the ice time. He suggested that I come in the month of December and coordinate my visit around an annual First Nations hockey tournament organized by members of the Esketemc First Nation. With that, plans were made to spend approximately two weeks in the community participating in the Esketemc Hockey Program, during which time I would provide a goaltending clinic and attend the Alkali Lake Braves adult hockey tournament.

Prior to my visit John provided me with a nine-page document outlining his First Nations hockey initiative to give me an idea of what to expect when I arrived. On receiving the document I was surprised to see that it was written by a consultant from Williams Lake, who was not of First Nations heritage but had extensive involvement in youth hockey. In the document the consultant writes that he is working from 'Johnny's idea for a First Nations Youth Hockey program' and that his 'input' had been sought 'to help develop such a program.' The program consists of three objectives: (1) to set up a youth hockey program, (2) to set up a coach recruitment and development program, and (3) to build an arena in Esket. People from Esket are currently forced to travel an hour by car to the nearest arena in Williams Lake, and since that arena serves all outlying areas, ice time is limited. Therefore, until the Esketemc First Nation can build an arena in their community, the program remains in the planning stage, where it has been since 2002.

News that the initiative was not yet up and running was confusing, because over the phone John had given me the impression that the program was already in place. If the program was not yet running, what would I be participating in during my stay, and why had I been invited to see it? I spoke to John two more times prior to going, but our conversations about the initiative created more confusion than clarity, so that by the time my two student research assistants and I arrived in early December, I did not know what to expect. We arrived at the small airport in Williams Lake and made arrangements to rent a car. While doing so, we noticed a First Nations gentleman and two adolescents standing alone, waiting in the airport. After a few minutes, the man approached me and shyly asked if I was Michael. John and his two sons drove into Williams Lake to greet us at the airport and assist us in getting to the community. I was touched by this gesture, which really set the tone for our stay in the community. We were warmly received and made to feel part of the community as soon as we arrived. Prior to leading us to the community, he suggested that we go out for supper at a restaurant in Williams Lake because he was not certain we would be able to get food in Esket by the time we arrived there. It was during supper that John revealed to me what his hockey initiative really was about and what he was trying to achieve with it.

At the restaurant John began telling us the history of the community and its struggles with alcohol abuse. Unlike the film's version, which emphasized the community's success in dealing with alcoholism, John's version of the story stressed the community's perpetual struggle to remain sober. His primary concern was the youth, who he felt did not have any structured activities available to them in their free time and were becoming increasingly vulnerable to substance abuse. He explained that during the evenings the kids would simply 'hang out' and were getting into trouble. He felt a hockey program would provide youth with something to do and prevent them from engaging in less-desirable activities, in particular experimenting with alcohol and drugs. Therefore, what was in place was essentially a weekly hockey game played at the arena in Williams Lake.

While listening to John describe the program, it conjured up notions of nineteenth century temperance movements in which sport and recreation were vehicles of social control. These kinds of initiatives, still being adopted today (Castellano and Soderstrom 1992; Iso-Ahola and Crowley 1991; McCann and Peters 1996; Spergel and Grossman 1997; Tindall 1995; Williams 1999; Wilson and Lipsey 2000), have, according to Varda Burstyn (1999), been utilized as preventive strategies against 'moral and physical turpitude' (56). In a somewhat typical mid-nineteenth-century program, the benefactors argued that 'the supervised public playgrounds and recreational Social Centre stimulate and guide a child's life in a way which no other factor of modern life can do' (Public Archives of Canada [PAC], No. MG 28 I 25, Vol. 105, File 10, quoted in Harvey 1988, 320). Important here is the suggestion that sport demonstrates desired behaviour, and in so doing directs youth away from participating in counterproductive or damaging behaviour. Through public demonstration and/or participation, specific actions are carried out that are deemed desirable, and for communities riddled with problems of substance abuse and disenfranchisement, these sport and recreation options appear attractive.

From what John was saying, it seemed that his program was simply capitalizing on mounting discourse about the need for First Nations youth to engage in positive and reaffirming leisure pursuits. In the 1995 *Report of the Royal Commission on Aboriginal Peoples*, an enormous document of over 3,500 pages, there are several occasions where community development and empowerment are connected to sport and recreation. At one point it reads, 'The absence of adequate recreation facilities and leisure activities is creating a pressing situation in many Aboriginal communities, where the large number of youth, their high and early school drop-out rates and the lack of jobs are a potentially explosive combination' (Indian and Northern Affairs Canada 1996, Volume 3.4). In Australia the Commission on Aboriginal Peoples reports that a strategy 'to reduce the demand for alcohol – particularly among young people – has been the provision of recreational activities' (Saggers and Gray 1998, 158). What is unique about many of the recreation programs for indigenous populations, in comparison to other more generic sport for development programs, is the emphasis on traditional cultural practices. For example, these initiatives in Australia extend beyond sport, calling also for an increase in traditional indigenous activities, which Saggers and Gray say provides a similar function. They write, 'there is a widespread and explicit acknowledgement of the importance of strengthening traditional culture and cultural values as a means of resisting excessive alcohol consumption' (ibid., 160). A similar strategy was employed in an alcohol treatment centre in Alberta, where a central component of the treatment program involved the 'strengthening and renewal of "Indian culture." An elder works full-time at the Centre, holding pipe ceremonies, sweat lodges, and other sacred ceremonies' (Hazlehurst 1994, 133). And again, like sport, it is the demonstrative capacity of these public cultural displays that makes them such useful means for behavioural persuasion, or, some might argue, social engineering.

For John, this notion of connecting sport to the culture was a fundamental component of his program. In our conversation he returned to the idea of the medicine wheel and how his program embodied the principles of emotional, physical, spiritual, and mental wellness. John explained that these four elements have become the guiding principles by which people from his community attempt to live their lives and achieve health and wellness. The idea of wellness in many North American indigenous societies is about balancing the multiple facets of existence, metaphorically articulated through the medicine wheel. Hillary Weaver (2002) explains that the wheel is broken into quadrants, each having 'layers of symbology' (6). She points out that quadrants can represent 'different spirit beings, the four directions . . . different stages of life, different races of people, different aspects within individuals, and different roles that people play within their community' (ibid., 7). The wheel connotes symmetry, representing the balance one needs in order to achieve wellness. And for John, his weekly hockey game was not merely a category of existence, but a means of striving towards personal development within a traditional Aboriginal framework. He said at one point:

> So that's what I'm trying to teach kids here, and a lot of it has to do with building self-esteem . . . A lot of them aren't going to make the big time but if I can build their self-esteem where they can go on to maybe become lawyers or doctors or even Indian Chief, that would be great. I mean that would be success . . . My program is organized around the four directions that we believe in – like the spiritual, emotional, physical, and mental – that's what I gear my programs towards, just developing these four areas.

The idea of incorporating First Nations culture into sport was interesting, but when I asked John how this specifically was to be done, he only provided vague responses about the youth being with the Elders and learning from them. It was not until my student and I eventually took part in the experience that the wonderful potential of such a program was made evident. I emphasize the word potential here, however, because the program was not fully implemented and had limited success in the community for a variety of reasons, which I will eventually speak to. First, I will describe the hockey program as we experienced it in hope of revealing the complexities of discipline, conformity, and border thinking that were displayed in the seemingly mundane expression of sport.

Learning to Prepare for Hockey

At the time of this research, the weekly hockey game was strategically scheduled for Saturday nights, the height of the weekend, and traditionally a night for socializing. In the Esketemc First Nation prior to the sobriety movement, 'there were drinking parties every weekend, often lasting for several days' (York 1989, 177). In York's study he quotes one member of the Esketemc community as saying, 'Every weekend you saw people walking around this whole reserve, people holding bottles and jugs and hollering' (ibid.). Therefore the hockey games on Saturday nights demonstrate a positive use of leisure time; a physical manifestation of the positive life messages the band currently advocates. The ice times, which had at one time involved drinking beer in the dressing room before and after the games – typical of adult recreational hockey in Canada – are now completely dry events. In speaking to the program's health director about this, she said:

> We ask them not to bring alcohol in the dressing rooms like they used to. And we've had a few people who complained but we said well you either come or you don't. And if you come here, this is what we expect. And some of the non-Native people were offended that we asked them not to drink but it's just how we run our programs.

Both John and the health director stressed the importance of role modelling and how important it was that the older guys provide a good example for the younger players. The health director pointed out that 'kids who have come through sports have had the support of their families and grow up to be really respectable adults. Whereas kids who never had that interaction and never participated in anything usually end up turning to drugs or alcohol and a lot of them ended up on the streets.' They also felt that through this positive interaction with the adults and youth, it revived traditional knowledge-sharing relations of First Nations cultures.

Our introduction to 'Saturday night hockey,' however, took place the night prior to the event on a Friday, because we were told we needed to prepare for the experience. To do so we were invited to participate in a sacred sweat lodge ceremony, which we were told would prepare us physically, mentally, emotionally, and spiritually for hockey. The sweat lodge had become part of the Saturday ritual, and players from the community as well as non-First Nation players would engage in these ceremonies prior to getting on the ice. The sweat lodge has become an important part of Esketemc culture since the sobriety movement in the 1970s. After generations of alcohol abuse and cultural dislocation as a result of the residential school system, the people of Esketemc had lost all traditional cultural practices. At the peak of the sobriety movement, Phyllis Chelsea, the woman who initiated the sobriety movement, sought help outside the community to restore indigenous practices. In *The Honour of All*, Phyllis narrates one scene, describing how she drove to Morley, Alberta, where medicine men were known to congregate. There she met Albert Lightning, a revered Elder and medicine man who agreed to visit the community and teach 'Native traditions.' In the film he is seen teaching the people how to make 'sacred sweat lodges,' something Phyllis 'had never heard of before.' Since then the community has embraced sweat lodge traditions, making the sweat lodge part of their daily lives. I had the opportunity to participate in both the sacred and more public sweat lodge ceremonies on two different occasions, each being tremendously moving experiences that I documented through field notes, though these notes pale to the experience itself.

On the night of the pre-hockey sweat lodge ceremony, we were invited to an Elder's home where his family prepared a meal for us. After the meal they brought us to the backyard where the sweat lodge was constructed. It was evening, and other than the fire burning outside the lodge it was dark. The Elder who was leading the ceremony explained to us very briefly that we were going to take part in four rounds of the sweat, each led with prayers, followed by chants and songs, and concluded with a brief cool down in the winter air and with water that was in barrels beside the fire. We entered the small rounded structure that was built from branches and covered in deer hides. The entrance was small, forcing us to crawl on our hands and knees to enter. Once inside, it was completely dark and we were guided by an Elder's voice who directed us where to crawl and sit so that we were huddled around the hot stones in the centre. The heat was intense, but not so overbearing that it was uncomfortable. There was a beautiful smell emanating from the rocks that were occasionally sprinkled with water and incense. Once we were all sitting in the darkness, we could hear the very gentle beating of the drum and the Elder singing quietly in his language. He then began a prayer in English giving thanks for all of us being there together and asking us if we had any special prayers we wanted to offer. We were later passed a stone, which, it was explained, served as a vessel for us to pray through. Somehow in the darkness it seemed easy to speak openly and offer prayers and give thanks, speaking to the stone carrying our prayer to whatever entities we were imagining. Once we were all done offering prayers, we were prompted to exit the sweat lodge and cool down in the sub-zero December air. Standing outside, barely clad bodies steaming and glistening by the fireside light, we joked with one another about the heat and how our bodies were responding. The Elder was pouring water over himself and rubbing his body down. Within minutes we went back into the lodge to go through another round. We eventually did this four times, the whole experience lasting about an hour. By the end of the ceremony I had a feeling of elation and light-headedness, but also calm. I wrote in my field notes afterwards:

We have gone through a sweat ceremony down on the property. It was intense and moving. We were fed, and then led down to the sweat lodge. Not too many words can describe it. It was the most intense experience I have ever had. What they showed me was compassion, honesty, and love. We shared in something very special. We prayed, we healed, and we laughed. It will be a memory I will never lose.

Having the opportunity to participate in a sacred sweat was special because of its formal, ritualized structure. I had the opportunity to participate in a less formal sweat the following year with another Elder who wanted to show my student and me how to make a sweat lodge and to share in what a more typical daily sweat involved. When I participated in the original sweat lodge ceremony I was uncertain about what I could record and what was private to the community, and have thus refrained from sharing some of the details. During the second sweat lodge experience I was more comfortable asking questions, since we had been invited for the express purpose of learning about the tradition. From this sweat I was able to put together a more detailed account of the experience, one that focuses on corporeal sensations and how this brought about a type of extraordinary awareness. It is important to describe this because of the centrality of the body in the sweat lodge experience, which is also key to the hockey experiences that were to follow. The following is an excerpt from my field journal summarizing the experience:

Last night my student and I participated in a sweat lodge ceremony with Richard and his brother Morris. We were supposed to head over to his place around 6:00 p.m. but we were given vague directions and ended up getting there a bit late. We seemed to be on the right path, but could not find what Richard told us to look for. We drove back down and on our right saw a huge fire in the middle of a field. We didn't know how to get down to it, partly because I was thinking it was going to be at a house like the sweat lodge I'd been to at Charles's place. We drove around for a while going nowhere and then decided to head back down to the store to ask directions. I was asking people where Richard lived, including some kids who we didn't know. They asked some of the adults inside and they said he lived with his dad, but we'd already been to his place and it wasn't it. So we were confused until we heard one of the kids say, 'Richard is here.' Sure enough his truck pulled up, looking for us at the hotel. It was close to 6:20 p.m. at this point, and while I was stressing because we were late, he was only just getting his towel and the sweat had not even started yet. He was still doing the preparations for the fire and the lodge itself. He told us to sit tight and he'd be back to get us in a few minutes.

We waited nearly twenty-five minutes for his return and followed him up the way we had originally gone. The reason we couldn't find his place on our own is because we were supposed to drive through a gate, which had not been open at the time. As we pulled through the gate, he waited in front of us for a few seconds, and I didn't know what he was doing. He got out of the car and I asked him if were parking here. He said, 'No, I have to close the gate.' I felt stupid, because that is what he was waiting for me to do, being the last person through the gate. He said, 'There's horses here.'

Sure enough, we started driving through the snow-covered field and there were about twenty horses roaming around. We got to the fire and sweat lodge, right down by the creek, and I realized this was going to be quite different than the sweat we had at Charles's place. It was probably about −10° Celsius, and we had no changing area. We were out in the open with the horses, the fire and the lodge.

Richard was getting the lodge prepared by pulling volcanic rocks out of the fire – they were red hot – and with a pitchfork placing them in the pit in the middle of the lodge. Some of the rocks were extremely heavy and it was difficult to get them up on the fork, balance them, and walk them over (about ten metres) to the lodge. Both my student and I helped him with this process in part to learn how it was done, but also because we were feeling useless standing there watching him work. It was apparent that the sweat lodge requires a lot of preparation and a lot of work. It requires hauling gallons of water up from the creek and chopping huge chunks of wood (over a metre long); the whole wood-gathering process is also physically demanding. The fires that are required for this are huge, burning upwards of two metres in diameter. A tremendous amount of wood is required, and considering that Richard and his brother sweat at least three times a week, a lot is needed to keep it going. On this note, there are about ten different sweat lodges in the area. There is one general area where the men and women sweat, albeit in different lodges. The elders go here as well. It's more of a public sweat. This sweat goes every day. Again, I was amazed at the amount work involved in making sure there is enough wood and water each day.

Once we had the rocks inserted into the pit in the lodge, the flap was closed and we had to wait for the lodge to heat up. We also had to wait for Richard's brother Morris to show up. Richard chopped some more wood and my student and I placed the wood on the fire that was beginning to dwindle. We built the fire up so that it was roaring once again, which is important for heat once we are done with the sweat, but also for heating the drum of water that sits right beside the fire. I'll explain this momentarily.

Morris arrived and we were pretty well ready to begin. Morris pried a small mat from the frozen ground and placed it next to the fire to thaw. He explained that the mat was important to stand on when we came out in between the sweats. Otherwise you stand on the snow and ice and freeze your feet. I scrambled to find my own mat, which turned out to be a rubber strip you might find at a hockey arena. It was still freezing cold, but more comfortable than standing on the snow.

The time came for us to disrobe and enter the lodge. Richard started to take off his clothes and explained that they usually do this naked, but said if we preferred we could leave shorts on. Wishing to follow what was typically done, we disrobed. Richard and Morris poured water on themselves prior to entering the lodge. My student and I refrained from pouring water over ourselves because we were already freezing. This was likely a mistake because the sweat lodge was hotter than we had anticipated. The idea is to be as cold as possible so the heat doesn't seem so bad when you get in. We climbed into the lodge, which was completely dark. You couldn't even see your hand in front of your face. There were also hot stones in the middle of a small space so we had to carefully crawl on our hands and knees to enter, led only by voices indicating where we were supposed to sit.

Once we all were settled inside, Richard began explaining aspects of the lodge, especially to my student who had never done this before. As we were sitting and talking, Richard would pour water on the rocks and the heat would become more intense. We were sitting on fir bows. They were surprisingly comfortable. It didn't take long before I was uncomfortably hot. I was starting to find the heat too much to take and was getting nervous that I was going to have to leave. I sat and tried to deal with the heat as best as I could. After talking, Richard began tapping his drum and began singing songs. He introduced each song as a prayer and explained its meaning. One was to the bear spirit; another was for travellers. As he sang, Morris would join in. They sang two songs per round. And as in the sacred sweat, we did four rounds of sweats. There was also incense put on the rocks that generated a sweet aroma. The effect was amazing. I'm not sure how long each sweat was, but after a period, Richard would say, 'ok, we'll go and cool off.' After the first round I was totally relieved to go outside as I was getting dizzy and feeling faint.

While outside we poured water over ourselves to wash away the sweat that was pouring out of our bodies. I couldn't believe how much sweat came out of me. It didn't take long though before our bodies were freezing once again. Richard sat on a bench. Morris stayed by the water barrels. My student sat down, and I just stood there feeling the freezing cold air on my body. It was an incredible feeling. My hair was actually freezing. It was a way of experiencing the elements that brings you as close to nature as humanly possible. Standing naked in the firelight was liberating. It is literally exposing yourself entirely, yet I didn't feel the least bit self-conscious. You have nothing to hide at that point.

We continued this process four times. Each time we entered the lodge we were colder than before. But after only a few minutes of the lodge, our bodies would reach a point of heat that was no longer endurable. The body would go through extremes that had an odd physical effect. I had been suffering from a cold for nearly two weeks and I wasn't sure if this would make things worse. Mucus was pouring out of me. They refer to the sweats as kind of cleansing, and without doubt, whatever was in me was being sweated out.

Over the course of the sweat, I learned that there are different kinds of sweats; some ceremonial, others more social. Although there were prayers through chants and singing, this sweat was social. The one I had experienced with Charlie was ceremonial. It was more ritualized with a formulaic prayer pattern. Here we could openly discuss the process and my student and I asked questions throughout.

Richard explained to us that it was here that visions would come to him. The songs he and his brother sang also came to him at these times. He said that the songs in the community were his creations. He has offered these songs to the community, and they are taken up by those who lead the sweats.

I asked him if the spirits came to this place. He said yes. He said sometimes you can see them. Other times you can hear them. He said he can sometimes hear someone swimming in the creek although there is no one else there. He said the spirits make their presence known. Without being an overly spiritual person, I did feel a connection to those around me that seemed to transcend basic human experience. I longed to do this with my own brother and I found myself really missing him. I commented on the closeness Richard and Charles must have since they do this together so often. Richard said this was one of the few times they had time to get together. They have to make a real effort to do this, which is evident as they go through the work to put on the sweat as many times as possible throughout the week.

Richard and Charles also talked about the public sweats and how they are conducted each night. On the weekends they often happen early in the morning. These are mostly for community members only, and visitors are brought to private sweats like Richard's, a little further away from the community. These public sweats often become competitions, Richard said. They are competitions in terms of the heat, trying to make it so hot to see who can last. But also in terms of storytelling – seeing who can outdo each other's stories.

They also talked about a time in the spring when they sweat from dusk until dawn; a dangerous proposition considering how much water is lost over the course of a single sweat. They drink water in between rounds to replenish the body. The sweats are clearly an important part of community life here. It is a time of connection. A time of healing. A time of communion. They have been doing this in the community for over twenty years. Richard said that the sweats have been part of Shuswap traditions according to Elders' stories.

In the field notes above I attempt to capture the intensity and intimacy of the experience. It was a type of awakening that had a profound impact on my student and me. Having the brothers walk us through the whole experience helped me to make sense of my initial sweat lodge experience the year before. At the conclusion of the original ceremonial sweat, the night prior to playing hockey, the Elder who performed the ceremony explained to us that we were now prepared to play hockey. He said that before all important games even the young children come to prepare according to the four guiding principles of mental, spiritual, physical, and emotional wellness. By sweating together, Elders and youth share in what they refer to as the interconnectedness of all aspects of life. In working, singing, dancing, or playing sport, the First Nation spirit is being expressed. In this regard, something as seemingly profane as hockey is at least rhetorically presented as a sacred and spiritual expression of self.

Deconstructing the Saturday Night Hockey Experience

It was in this context that Esketemc hockey was introduced. My students and I were told to arrive at the Williams Lake arena around

8:00 p.m. to take part in the game. When we arrived I was surprised that hardly anyone was there. We entered the dressing room and there were only three other guys there. Some had full hockey equipment, others, like my student and me, only had skates, gloves, and a stick. As we sat there waiting for people to show up, there was little conversation. As we got dressed, no one seemed particularly interested in who we were, so we simply put on our skates and went out thinking that there were likely already more skaters on the ice. To our surprise there was only one other person, a woman who had changed in the other dressing room. We skated around shooting and passing the puck, waiting for the rest of the players to come out. By the time John came out there were only eight skaters, which is not enough to have an actual game. To make things worse, there were no goalies. Without enough players, I assumed people might just skate around and shoot pucks for a while and then leave, but instead a makeshift game broke out.

The game consisted of a five on three scrimmage, with the team with extra players putting one person in goal. Partway through the game, about five younger players (between fifteen and twenty years old) came out so we could make the teams more even. With the extra players, a four on four scrimmage game emerged, with one goalie and one extra guy on each bench. Without goalies, outside shots were not allowed, which meant you had to go around people and the goalie before putting the puck in the net. The intention was to dangle[2] with the puck and score with the goalie deaked[3] out of his net. This emphasis on individual flair is something I've noticed in other First Nations hockey games, where the dangle is the most praised hockey quality. Here, a couple of guys, young and old, could put the puck to their feet and back to the stick, which seemed to be their favourite move.

The game lasted for nearly two hours and there was no sign of anyone losing interest. In fact some people from the community came out to watch, cheer, laugh, and take pictures. They seemed to be enjoying the game as much as the players. One of the Elders from the community came to watch and it was evident how happy he was seeing this makeshift game take place. He cheered and banged on the glass, and everyone on the ice was aware of his presence. It was a showcase of talent,

---

2 To dangle is to creatively stickhandle the puck in order to bypass other players or score on the net.
3 To deak in hockey is to go around an opponent while maintaining control of the puck.

with players proudly performing their skills in front of their community. At the end of the game, the dressing room was much more active and guys came up to my student and me saying that we should play for their team. Only then did they formally introduce themselves and welcome us to their game. It was a really nice feeling. We sat around chatting while getting undressed, and eventually got some team photos taken.

What I have just described here is what constitutes the hockey program. The games are highly enjoyable for players and for the few regular spectators who watch their friends and relatives play against one another. It has become a Saturday night ritual, a symbolic text that speaks to the struggles and triumphs the community has endured since the move towards sobriety. The richness of this text, however, is not likely appreciated when analysed as a mere pick-up hockey game. To appreciate the significance of what is taking place, we must return to what I alluded to earlier as the prescriptive and regimented elements of sport, which have made it such a desirable means of modifying behaviour. It conscripts bodies not only to perform in specific ways, but also prevents participants from engaging in other more harmful leisure pursuits. Sport has been construed as healthful, positive physical activity that wields a type of control over participants, subordinating them to the tenets of play and to controlling forces of society. What is most appealing in this dynamic of power is the *willing* subjugation of participants (though for youth it is parents placing them in a position of subjugation) to the prescriptive and disciplining techniques of sport. A performance-based sport ethic has overshadowed even the most grassroots levels of sport, where results-based programs demand competitiveness and professionalism.

A humorous television commercial speaks to the seemingly innocuous yet insidious pervasiveness of this naturalized construct of sport. In this commercial, advertising sport merchandise, we see a recreational hockey player decked out in high-end gear skating off the ice. He is met by a woman who appears to be his wife or girlfriend. She says, 'Great game!' and he responds by delivering an interview-like response that has become standard during professional hockey television broadcasts: 'We need to keep working hard out there, moving the puck . . .' The woman gives him a bewildered look and asks him what he is talking about. He continues in interview mode, only to have her say, 'Mike, I'll be in the car.' A caption appears below that reads, 'Dress like a pro, act like a pro,' advertising brand-name sportswear for pro-minded hockey players without pro-hockey salaries or abilities.

The commercial captures the far-too-frequent misguided sensibilities of modern sport, but also provides an interesting commentary on the influence of professional sport on everyday sporting practices. These influences, humorously displayed here, carry with them serious consequences for those interested in the realm of leisure and the constraints and coercions to which people are subjected, and/or subject themselves, in their free time. In fact the automatic interview mode of the recreational hockey player is a clever depiction of the athlete as automaton, a disciplined body performing tasks efficiently, effectively, and thoughtlessly, achieving what Michel Foucault (1977) has described as docility. This disciplinary framework of sport makes it popular for those wishing to impose social control or reform, yet it has drawn criticism from sport scholars who point to the levels of control sport exercises over the body and over the societies who endorse them.

In this regard I wish to draw attention to the work of Pierre Bourdieu and Michel Foucault and their theorizing of the body as the subject of domination and control. It has been long taken for granted that sport in its modernized form has served as an important socializing agent, developing what ruling classes have understood to be important individual and nationalistic qualities, such as leadership, discipline, character, and general fitness. For Bourdieu (1988), however, the body itself becomes central to this disciplining process in that the voluntary compliance to sporting behaviours achieves a kind of 'methodological manipulation of the body' that serves as a form of consent to domination that the mind may otherwise reject (161). The imposition of ruling-class designs on what were once unruly and self-gratifying physical pastimes means that participation in modern sport becomes a means to 'somatize the social by symbolizing it, and aim at reinforcing social orchestration through its bodily and collective mimesis' (ibid.). According to Richard Gruneau (1993) this was part of a public design to create a new moral order based on ideas of 'rationality, discipline, health, bodily prowess, and masculine loyalty' (90), and sport, in its institutionalized framework, is a primary means of orchestrating what are essentially bodily symbolizations of these fundamental notions.

For Foucault (1977) the emphasis shifts from locatable relations of power orchestrating and imposing social control to the body as agent in the production of power, and the means by which this is achieved. Like Bourdieu, Foucault understands the body as a critical site in the production of power, but Foucault differs in that he believes that the body's complicitous response to disciplines of subjugation enters it into power relations, not merely situating it as the object of control and domination. This twofold process is discussed through the notion of docility, which he explains as 'disciplinary coercion [that] establishes in the body the constricting link between an increased aptitude and an increased domination' (138). In other words, as bodies are methodologically manipulated (to borrow from Bourdieu) the body becomes increasingly efficient and ultimately more useful. There is an even greater insidiousness to this 'mechanics of power' than the somatized body of Bourdieu, in that the more disciplined the body becomes, the greater its use or value in larger socio-economic relations. Disciplinary control then means having 'a hold over others' bodies, not only so that they may do what one wishes, but so that they may operate as one wishes, with the techniques, the speed and the efficiency that one determines' (ibid.).

The impact both of these theorists have had on the study of sport has been significant, in that the body becomes the direct focus for which disciplinary strategies, or technologies of the self, unfold. Sport is seen as a literal expression of bodily submission to rules and regulations, and to the physical moves and postures of the athletic performance. Subjecting oneself to the disciplines which have been grossly standardized by sport experts ensures proficiency, and thus subjugation to these authorities is not only tolerated, but desired (which is nicely explored in Shogan's [1999] book *The Making of High Performance Athletes*). It is this proficiency, this sporting excellence, that carries such profound symbolic value in that mastery over one's body is seen as enabling, productive, and desirable. The athletic body becomes the model of discipline, something to strive for, and those who do not achieve this model are undisciplined, lazy, unproductive, and unwanted. The once wonderfully hedonistic impulses that gave way to sporting practices have been erased by a wilful subjugation to sporting authorities to enhance one's effectiveness in what is in reality a completely unproductive domain. Yet these disciplining effects remain, carrying with them a self-regulating potential that Jeremy Bentham couldn't have envisioned with the most efficient of panopticons.

My interest in the notion of the panopticon is the manner in which 'modern societies [sport in particular] utilize a disciplinary power based on a system of surveillance that is internalized to such an extent that each person now becomes his or her own overseer' (Rail and Harvey 1995, 166). The disciplinary controls that have come to shape sporting practices have been so successful that participants measure their own worth through these disciplinary standards. Critical here is the voluntary submission to modes of surveillance that debilitate the expressive and liberating potential of sport. David Whitson (1984) has written extensively on this phenomenon, which he explains has 'reinforce(d) the "naturalness" of disciplined and achievement-oriented structures of feeling' (69). To see an illustration of this, one need only go to an Atom hockey game in Canada and watch the nine- to ten-year-old children arrive wearing shirts and ties, aping the business model of sport that shapes not only their attire, but the overly competitive environment of youth hockey. My own research on hockey in Canada testifies to this, as the excessive structuring of hockey, even at the grassroots levels, coerces athletes to the most finite levels of control (Robidoux 2001; Robidoux and Trudel 2006). For this reason, sports such as hockey are used as disciplining devices in which participants wilfully engage. The consequence is that participants, even in the most recreational sense, engage in these behaviours, shaping how they come to 'play.'

For First Nations communities, there is a double effect here in that sport may serve as a tool of assimilation, prompting participants to engage in Western-based activities, which in turn devalues local cultural practices. Using sport as an assimilatory strategy demands that participants obey the rules and structure of the game in order to achieve any level of competency. For example, to engage in the most basic tasks required in playing hockey, whether skating or shooting the puck, great demands are placed on the body. To return briefly to Foucault, this is most evident in his notion of the 'body-object articulation,' which he describes as 'the instrumental coding of the body' (1977, 153). It is a category of disciplinary power that unfolds in two parallel phases, where the body is organized in relation to its own physical comportment, and simultaneously to the objects manipulated to meet the sporting end. Foucault describes this process in terms of a soldier, but the same can be said about sport, in which participants are required to achieve outcomes through the materials the sporting structure provides. In this regard, Foucault's soldier analogy is most relevant: 'Over the whole surface of contact between the body and the object it handles, power is introduced, fastening them to one another. It constitutes a body-weapon, body-tool, body-machine complex' (ibid.). In the game of hockey, athletic efficacy is contingent on this body-object complex in that tools of the sport are extensions of the athletic gestures. To skate one needs to manipulate the body and skate in such a manner as to produce force, and as the following example illustrates, the mechanics of the act have been meticulously broken down:

During the glide phase the body is supported over one leg that remains at nearly a constant length (ankle to hip distance). The push-off phase begins with the initiation of leg extension and ends near full leg extension when the skate blade lifts off the ice. The skate is returned to the initial position under the body during the recovery phase which begins at the end of the push-off phase and ends when the blade contacts the ice . . . During this period, body weight is transferred from the push-off skate to the gliding skate. (Allinger and Van Den Bogert 1997, 279)

By the simple execution of this one task (and obviously this is only one of the many combinations of movements that participants must adhere to) it is evident how bodies are shaped not only by the dictates of sport, but also by the object themselves that enable or disable proficiency. It is this instrumental coding, which has become so naturalized in modern athletics, that shapes the manner in which sport is seen and experienced by the vast majority of its participants.

This analysis, however, is largely unidirectional and does not account for the deconstructive potential that lies in bodies, in this case bodies of the colonized, taking up modern sport. In the introduction I mentioned C.L.R. James's struggles to embrace but also reinvent sport. The local manipulations of sport he describes are not unlike those in the Esketemc First Nation, where the suggestion of an assimilatory effect of sport (in this case hockey) was adamantly rejected. In fact, comments in a personal interview conducted with the Chief of the Esketemc First Nation were reminiscent of what was put forth by James:

ROBIDOUX: There have been people who have argued that modern sport was introduced as an assimilation strategy. For example, even hockey, it was introduced in the residential schools?
CHIEF: Yes.
ROBIDOUX: Do you see that as a threat to culture? Or do you see it as a way of empowering a culture through sport?
CHIEF: I think it's an enhancing tool. I think it's just – you have to remember, a long time ago, even in the east, the Six Nations people had lacrosse and stuff like. It has a lot of similarity [to hockey], you see? And also we had our own sports on horseback that might be understood along with hockey. So I don't see it as assimilation if we do it in a better way, huh.

The mastery over sport that James and the Esketemc Chief are referring to is one method of resistance or manner in which colonial designs can be turned on their head. In many international sporting contexts, such as cricket and soccer, the colonized are now the leaders of the sport, and the colonizer is striving to catch up (for example, see Wagg 2005).

Conversely, this mastery can be interpreted as the perfect illustration of docility, which does not mean passivity but rather giving one's self up in order to be made pliable, disciplined, and in turn highly proficient. For a sporting culture to master and ultimately dominate a sport suggests an unequivocal level of docility to not only the sport regimen, but to Western constructs of structure, progress, competition, and winning. During my fieldwork playing hockey in the Esketemc First Nation, however, I did not witness the disciplining measures so typically encountered in organized sport. Hockey in this community provided an alternative model of resistance that achieved a type of ownership over the sport without capitulating to the modernist designs of progress and rationalization. The oppositional framework found here was interestingly achieved through the body-object articulation, or rather the breakdown of this articulation. Instead of a highly structured and regimented style of play, hockey in this context displayed an ad hoc relationship of bodies and tools that produced inefficient and unstructured displays of sport. The lack of players, positions, equipment, and so on exemplified the inability of bodies and objects to mesh, undermining any 'explicit and obligatory prescriptions' (Foucault 1977, 153) sport might offer. In this context, it was the undertaking of bringing bodies and objects together that made hockey so desirable, not the performative outcomes that this body-object complex is intended to produce. Having played organized hockey throughout my life, participating in this event produced a defamiliarizing effect, where I had to renegotiate my bodily competence (or perceived competence) in this new environment. After playing hockey that Saturday night, I attempted to capture the experience in my field notes:

Bodies of various shapes, sizes, and capabilities began putting on an equally motley assortment of equipment: new skates followed by broken shin pads, torn hockey pants, or in some cases jeans. A Montreal Canadiens jersey was pulled over one body, covering what appeared to be hole or scar on his stomach, inflicted, I figured, by a knife wound. Cigarettes were smoked by some, while others applied tape to the remains of hockey sticks. Sporadically, people exited the dressing room and got onto the ice.

On this particular day there are no goalies, and at the outset not enough play-ers to have six per side. No teams are picked, nor are coloured jerseys matched to play against light jerseys. The game simply begins with players on one side moving towards an empty net, while others attempt to prevent a goal from oc-curring. Oddly, I found myself completely lost on the ice. With some players barely able to skate, and others taking the puck attempting to go end-to-end and score on a relatively unguarded net, it was difficult to know how to react. I began passing the puck off as soon as I got it, but was quickly heckled by an older guy for not burying (finishing) my chance. It took time to recognize that it was simply about playing, which I had difficulty adjusting to. It made me feel self-conscious, as if I was exposing something highly personal, like letting someone in on my imagination. But I slowly began to play with the others and became highly cognizant of the intimacies of the game that I had either forgotten or never really paid attention to. Taking the puck on the stick and cradling it, taking long strides and feeling your blades cut through the ice, feeling the air on your face as you pick up speed, feeding someone the puck; all of these things be-came intimately experienced, and sharing these sensations in this context was fulfilling. For nearly two hours we skated, and as the Zamboni doors opened we stopped playing and began leaving the ice. We returned to our dressing room with sweat-drenched bodies, disrobed, and shared in the collective banter. It was a hockey formula that I have been encountering for nearly forty years, but it was practiced in a manner that I had never before experienced.

The subversion I am associating with the Saturday night hockey game is not something John intended in designing the program. In fact, John openly expressed that his idea for designing it was to provide youth with structured positive experiences to prevent them from using drugs and alcohol, but also to provide youth with opportunities to 'make it.' While making it did not necessarily mean making it to profes-sional hockey, sport was clearly construed as a means for advancement, whether providing youth with opportunities to go to college or univer-sity, or to help carve out a path for future success. Sport is perceived as a means to an end, which is a mentality that dominates the Western world of organized sport. It is for this reason that adult-based sport frameworks are privileged over unorganized youth activities, in that sport must somehow be productive to be valuable, an idea that has per-meated even the most local sensibilities. John said to me at one point,

A lot of these guys that play on our Saturday nights have been playing forty years. So a lot of skills that were picked up, like even with John [his son], have been from coming out with our old timers since he was about eleven or twelve. So I'm trying to get the old timers to be role models to young people and show them the skills they had when they played hockey.

The positive outcome John ascribes to his son's playing hockey with the Elders speaks to what I would argue is a more meaningful experience than what was initially intended. The hockey program is an opportunity for intergenerational and intercommunity sharing, a uniquely local experience that is open to members outside of the community, but local in design and practice. It is an expression of the community and the culture, transcending any assimilatory or subjugating designs. It is a type of border gnosis, where we see the local engaged with the global, producing its own meaningful exchange. The unique expression of sport exposes cracks in the dominant Western imaginary, in that it reveals what the community Chief once explained to me: 'Sport is, I call it the esteem of First Nations Spirit. It's just the spirit explaining itself, you know, of a life.'

These local meanings were vividly expressed to me in an interview with a woman who had learned that I was conducting research about hockey in the community and wanted to share with me a story about her grandson and nephew's son playing hockey in Williams Lake. The story, which I provide below, is informative not only in terms of its content, but also in the manner in which it is told. Its disjointed narrative style destabilizes comprehension, forcing the listener to follow intently what is being said. It also exposes its distinctiveness as a local narrative articulated along the borders of First Nations and Euro-Canadian experience. Through its performance it achieves what Homi Bhabha (1991) describes as redefining the signifying relation of signs, reinscribing meaning into local hockey experiences. I have provided a verbatim transcript of the narrative, editing for clarity at points only when absolutely necessary.

I have two boys that I take to hockey. Um, I'm not even hockey oriented, nothing. But I have this grandson since he was four weeks old and he was born with a cleft palate. And so I have ended up raising him. When he was four, he started talking. And I have another, my nephew's son, that also started hockey. My grandson wasn't too interested and I ended up going and taking him just to practices. But nobody was taking the other boy. So my grandson, he used to tell me that Kenneth was crying; nobody would take him to hockey. So I just decided,

I decided that I would just start taking him. So for years now, I've been taking them to Williams Lake. Um, and I guess about the same time too, they were four when my father, um, committed suicide. And these two boys really liked my dad. He used to always like to watch hockey, like he would travel to Williams Lake a long time ago and watch the Stampeders. And he would listen to the radio when I was a kid, listen to hockey because we didn't have TV. So he was really into hockey and those boys knew it, they grew up around him. And he used to sit outside and I remember he used to have a goalie stick and he used to let them shoot at him. That's how I remember; he was always doing something for them. So when [she sighs] he, he committed suicide and he was poor – so it's four years past because they're eight and the other one just turned nine. And we were at hockey just recently, I think two weekends ago. We had to be there by eight o'clock. Um, leave at six thirty I think and we were there for an eight o'clock game. And there were three boys that didn't show up. So my friend's son, he was never goalie before but he said he'd go in net. And there were only two First Nations I think on this team. And anyway he was never goalie before and he wouldn't get down on the ice; he would just stand there with his stick. He was just scared to get set. He was telling me this later. But anyway, my other grandson, he's smaller than him. He's older but small built and every time his line got off, only three kids would get on and he would stay out on the ice. And he played the whole time and I knew he was tired. I couldn't stand it. I went out twice because I couldn't watch. So I came back and I kept thinking why can't they just call the game because I know that my little guy was tired. But they played and they lost like 5–3. But he would skate down, he would skate back and he, he would look after Jason. But I didn't realize he was doing that; that's what he told me. I think that I could afford to go to a new hockey school – he was starting to use the skills. He would shoot the puck to the side, and go around the players. And he started passing. Before he wasn't doing that – he would bring it in and try to score – he was passing, he was starting to use everything he learned. And after the game was over, we went into the dressing room, and Kenneth just dropped himself on his back and said, 'My legs!' Because he always has aching legs, but he likes to play. And then we left and we were in the car and, and um, Jason, told me, 'You know I, I, I saw Pa7a.' [pronounced Pa-a; Secwepemc word for grandfather]. That's what he called my dad. And I said, 'Oh yeah?' And Kenneth said, 'Yeah, I saw him there too. He was standing on the side watching us.' And I said, 'Oh yeah?' And Jason said 'Yeah he was there watching us.' And I said 'Oh, what did he do? Did he say anything? Did he do anything?' And Jason said 'He came to me and he told me to put my hands down to the ice and cover the puck.' Jason told him, 'But I'm scared. I won't be able to get the puck.' And he said, 'But he stayed, he stayed there and he was watching.' And the boys said, 'Do you know what that means?' He said, 'He has come to watch us.' And so they were all excited. And they said,

'We never seen him for a long time since we were, since he died,' he said. 'We saw him then but we never seen him since he died.' So they were all excited. But they said also, 'Whenever we go somewhere, we know he can be there, he can get there anywhere in the world.' Because they've gone to only the one tournament last year and they won in Prince George; so they're just starting out.

After the story concluded I asked the woman how common such an experience was, and she replied, 'Usually we could go out fasting for days, but for the boys, with all the praying – when we say praying it means they go to the sweat lodge – they pray to their grandfather. I think that's what they thought, like he's letting us know like, he's there, and he's okay.'

There are several important themes that are evident in this narrative, the first being the suicide itself. As mentioned earlier, the community has undergone incredible suffering as a result of alcoholism, sexual abuse, domestic violence, and the residential school system. For some people, suicide has been a tragic response to these overwhelming circumstances and has been one more thing with which the community has had to contend over the past thirty years. Discovering ways to recover from these tragic circumstances has been at the forefront of the community since the sobriety movement, and as shown here, people have turned to practices they identify with First Nations culture, such as sweat lodges and fasting. What is highly noteworthy is that the boys are reunited with their deceased grandfather during a hockey game, where he demonstrates that he is forever watching over them. Hockey was something their grandfather loved and in turn becomes a place where he can transcend the boundaries of life and death to express his love for his grandsons. This is a story about healing and it is through hockey that healing is made possible. Through this narrative, the sport of hockey becomes reconstituted into local cultural practices, reinscribed with local meanings and knowledge. It is reconstituted just like the sweat lodge and fasts, which were introduced to the community by an Elder at the height of the sobriety movement. They have become part of their own history, retold and reconfigured in a turbulent present. For this reason, hockey can be part of the ongoing healing process, not in the conformist assimilatory context in which it was initially introduced to First Nations peoples, but as a meaningful cultural experience. It was here that the meaningfulness of hockey was made possible, far beyond the capacities of what any program could deliver, and far beyond anything I could have envisioned.

Afterthoughts

My serendipitous involvement with the Esketemc First Nation provided unanticipated experiences and insights into local cultural
practices. The importance of hockey was made clear to me, but after
learning more about the community, it was more understandable. Over
the course of my fieldwork I encountered another Alkali Lake story
that is less known internationally, but more celebrated, at least among
the local people. This story is about a 1930s hockey team from the Esketemc First Nation, which gained notoriety for being the best hockey
team in the region. In almost all my conversations with people about
the sport, they would make reference to this team as part of an almost-
forgotten but proud history. In *Dog Creek: A Place in the Cariboo*, Hilary
Place (1999) provides one of the more detailed accounts of the heroic
team that garnered so much success in interior British Columbia and
was invited to play a senior hockey team in Vancouver to challenge
them for western hockey supremacy. Chase describes it as follows:

> None of the Alkali Lake men had even been to the big city. They had never
> played on artificial ice in a stadium and they had also never played, or
> seen, for that matter, a professional hockey player . . . The players came
> dressed in their normal working attire: buckskin gloves and coats, blue
> jeans, cowboy hats, and boots. The Vancouver papers were full of pictures
> and write-ups about them. (71)

The team from Alkali Lake ended up losing both games by a single goal
despite predictions of being routed. The team, which was undefeated in
the interior region, had no real hockey experience. They were a bunch of
ranch hands who were introduced to the sport by the local rancher who
wanted them to be kept occupied during the slower winter months. They
often travelled over nine hours in one direction for a game, and slept in
tents while away. When news came that they pushed this team of all-stars
to the limit during the two-game exhibition, they became hockey legends.
Some of the players were offered professional hockey tryouts, but all ended
up returning to their home community. Place, a British expat who played
hockey for the neighbouring community of Dog Creek, fondly remembers
playing in Alkali Lake a few years after the Vancouver showdown:

> As our team at Dog Creek improved, we began playing the Alkali team
> quite a bit. Their love of the game still showed, and it inspired us to play

our best. Their rink was out in the open air in the Indian village at Alkali Lake, and a big fire always burned alongside the sheet of ice where we sat to put on our skates. All the people from the reserve, about a hundred of them, gathered around talking and laughing and enjoying themselves, along with a few whites. (ibid., 74–5)

During my fieldwork in Esket, people still talked about this team. The history being shared was not only about the hockey team, but also about a more positive period in the community's history. When people told their stories about the team they would also make reference to the era, which they described as the pre-drinking period when people were physically active, strong, and healthy. In an interview I conducted with a man who was the grandson of the goaltender for this famous team, he explained that 'this was a different way of life' that necessitated physical fitness. He talked about the hunt, transportation, and labour on the ranch, which were extremely physically demanding. He said, 'They had to be in shape. They didn't have a choice.' During my conversation with him, he took out some pictures he had of the team and held them in his hand while talking to me. I eventually asked him what happened to the team. As the team was linked to an era, so too was their demise, which he linked to the introduction of the residential schools. He described it as 'as a loss of childhood'; when he and the rest of the children came out, 'they were angry and lost.' Many, he said, turned to alcohol, and 'hockey was lost with this, as was the rest of their childhood.' He described it as a dark age, and whatever connection they had to the past was severed, including hockey.

The past, however, has not been severed, but reconfigured. The heroic status of the Alkali Lake hockey team has remained strong and something community members recite as a testament to their community's strength and perseverance. They too, like the hockey team, have overcome the odds and achieved success after what were their darkest hours. In reconfiguring the past, its signification can also be altered; this is evident in the interview I conducted with the woman who told me about her grandson's experience with her father's spirit. In the interview I found out that her uncle played for the famed Alkali Lake team and that her mother told her about how her uncle 'used to get up really early in the morning, go to the sweat lodge like five o'clock in the morning, go to sweat before they went out.' The likelihood of the 1930s hockey team performing sweats prior to getting on the ice is slim considering the Roman Catholic restrictions the community was living under at that time. Moreover, in the film *The Honour of All*, Phyllis Chelsea openly states that she had never heard of such a thing as a sweat lodge prior to visiting the medicine man in Morley, Alberta. With this said, the tenuous relationship with the past enables such reconfigurations, which in turn lead to reconstitutions of the present. Hockey serves as an inspirational tale from the past, one that is being reconjured in the present, whether in the form of loosely structured intergenerational pick-up hockey, or in the more competitive elite leagues that more and more youth from the community are entering.

While in interior British Columbia, I had the opportunity to witness these more elite expressions of First Nations hockey, in part through observing First Nations hockey tournaments, and also watching individual First Nations people playing junior hockey in the region. It is here that the next stage of research unfolds, which presents a vastly different image of First Nations hockey than what I experienced participating in the Esketemc Hockey Program. This is not to say that more structured and organized forms of First Nations hockey are devoid of the qualities observed in Esket, but their practices are more closely tied to Euro-Canadian/Western norms, so the cracks are at times more difficult to see. From these cracks we can begin examining the multifaceted and multivalent phenomenon of First Nations hockey tournaments to decipher the potential points of enunciation and meaning-making that have made these events such important sites for community celebration for over thirty years.

3 First Nations Hockey Tournaments: Celebrating Culture through Sport

ROBIDOUX: Hey Harley, why isn't there an A division in this tournament?
HARLEY: Oh, that's because in school a B is a Native A.

The description provided of hockey in the Esketemc First Nation was intended to expose the powerful potential sport has as local cultural practice. The value in this case was identified in the manner in which it destabilized dominant Western sporting practices that embody the tenets of modernity: rationalization, technological advancement, and progress. It is important to state, however, that hockey in the Esketemc First Nation is not necessarily representative of First Nations hockey in general; there are many forms of First Nations hockey, with various levels of skill, organization, and competitiveness. What was relatively consistent throughout this research was the passion with which First Nations peoples have embraced the sport across the country. To gain an appreciation for this diversity of experiences and expressions of First Nations hockey, I decided to focus on First Nations tournaments over a three-year period from 2002 to 2005. This decision was based on the relative importance of these tournaments as critical sites to experience hockey, whether as a player, coach, manager, sponsor, organizer, volunteer, fan, family member, or a combination of the above.

These tournaments are the most prominent public displays of adult First Nations hockey and continue to hold a special significance for many First Nations peoples and communities across the country. They also reveal much about the intersections of local and global sport designs, especially as the tournaments are becoming higher profile events with increased commercial and economic capacity. The tournaments for some are slowly embodying professional hockey standards and becoming less connected to First Nations culture and identity. There are other community-based events that run counter to high-performance athletic standards and sensibilities, yet tend to be marginalized by marquee First Nations tournament players as illegitimate, 'backwoods' forms of hockey. What will follow, then, is an examination of these tensions as First Nations hockey publicly defines itself within the modern colonial imaginary. In this chapter I will focus on both the more professional tournaments and a local community-based First Nations tournament to illustrate two very different points. In terms of the professional tournaments, I offer analysis focusing on processes of accommodation and subversion that make each of these tournaments distinctive, yet still seemingly meaningful to the people and communities who celebrate them. I discuss the community-based tournaments as manipulations of Western standardized hockey practices, and point to the particular importance these tournaments have for First Nations peoples living in more remote and rural regions of Canada.

As I begin to discuss these two types of tournaments – high-performance versus more community-based – I am not making an evaluative comment on existing tournament play, or attempting to provide a classification system of tournaments. When I refer to tournaments that are more professionalized, high-performance events, I am speaking about tournaments that do not require players to play with their own communities to participate. In contrast, community-based tournaments require players to play for their own band (or First Nation) as defined by their registration status with Indian and Northern Affairs Canada. In the high-performance tournaments, players are required to be Aboriginal as defined by the Indian Act,[1] yet are not required to play with their registered bands. Teams are therefore made up of the best possible Aboriginal players, regardless of their ancestral background. The teams themselves typically originate out of a single community, yet often have few if any members from the actual band playing on the team. A local team organizer puts the team together by recruiting the best possible players, creating highly competitive teams. Tournaments that require players to play with their own communities have a smaller

---

1 See 'Indian Registration System/Certificate of Indian Status' as defined by Indian and Northern Affairs Canada (http://www.ainc-inac.gc.ca/gol-ged/faq_e.html).

talent pool to draw from and typically are unable to compete with the 'all-star' teams in open tournaments.

Therefore, the recruitment process in non-band-specific tournaments is the key to competitive success. A combination of networking skills and available funds is essential for assembling competitive teams. It is in this capacity that these high-profile tournaments distinguish themselves from local tournaments, as they have gradually become semi-professional in that hired players are paid for their services to perform over the course of the event. The professional framework has ultimately established a network of players for hire who participate in a tournament circuit that spans the country throughout the fall and winter months. Thus the distinction I am making between tournaments is based on this professionalized framework, not purely on the level of play itself. I point this out because I have witnessed over the course of this fieldwork highly competitive band-based teams that were capable of playing in professionalized tournaments, and band-based tournaments that were highly skilled events. The professionalized events, however, function much differently and have aligned themselves more closely with dominant sporting practices in Canada, prompting distinctive analytic commentary. I will begin by focusing on the larger performance-based tournaments and my fieldwork accounts of these events.

High Performance Tournaments

As mentioned in the introduction to this book, my involvement in prominent First Nations hockey tournaments was made possible through Don Jones, a friend and former hockey teammate's brother who was still actively playing in the First Nations hockey circuit. Don had been playing First Nations tournament hockey for over fifteen years and suggested that I build my fieldwork schedule around the tournaments he would play in over the 2002–2004 hockey seasons. I ended up visiting three different tournaments, attending each one twice, over the course of two seasons. I will provide summaries of each of the tournaments and then provide analytic commentary about my experiences observing tournament play and participating in tournament events.

Brandon

The first major tournament I attended was held in Brandon, Manitoba, in January 2003 and 2004. The first year the event was called the First

Nation Winter Celebration, but in 2004 its name changed to Winter Tribal Days, and it was advertised as 'Canada's Largest Aboriginal Event.' While I am not able to attest to it being the largest Aboriginal event in Canada, it was certainly the largest First Nations hockey event I attended throughout my fieldwork. This is not to say that it was the largest event because of the hockey, but rather because of the myriad activities that were concurrently offered, making it much more than a hockey tournament. The event was quite distinctive in that it was more of a winter festival with hockey as one of the primary attractions rather than being a standard tournament. The venue was also distinctive in that it was held at a modern multifunctional complex that had three ice surfaces, conference and meeting rooms, and a variety of multipurpose rooms – some large enough to accommodate tractor and agriculture shows. When the event was established in the early 1970s it was simply a hockey tournament, but with the creation of the Keystone Centre Complex, it afforded tournament organizers the opportunity to expand beyond hockey and offer additional attractions. The tournament organizers, initially the Dakota Ojibway Tribal Council and now the Sioux Valley Dakota First Nation, recognized that the event was a valuable means of bringing people together – males and females of all ages – and in turn started accommodating this diversity by providing activities for people who were not solely interested in or capable of playing hockey. In an interview conducted with the 2004 tournament organizer, he explained that 'this is a very unique facility. There isn't another place like this in Canada. The majority of the people who come, come for the hockey. When I started in about 1982, 1983 . . . we noticed that there were a lot of kids running around, basically unsupervised. You had older people that really didn't watch the hockey, so we started having different events. So now there's always something for someone to do.' Since that time, the event has grown so that in addition to the hockey, which comprises youth, female, 'old-timers,' recreational, and competitive divisions, there are fifteen other attractions for people to enjoy. Recently a partial list of the activities included craft exhibitions, pow wow competitions, the First Nation Princess Pageant, a Much Music video party, a fiddling competition, the Moccasin Game,[2] monster bingo, arm

---

2 There are many varieties of the traditional Anishnawbe moccasin game, but at
   the Brandon tournament, it is played with two individuals sitting across from one
   another. One player has a stone or small bone and tries to hide it under a series of

wrestling, a talent show and jigging competition, square dance competitions, professional wrestling with former WWF star Tatanka,[3] and a strongman competition. Activities that were listed as competitions advertised a range of prize money, for example, $1,000 for first place in the square dance and $75 for first place in fiddling. Admission into the arena complex was $12 per day for adults and each of the events required entrance fees to participate.

The hockey component of the tournament was slightly modified from 2003 to 2004. In 2003 there were more youth divisions, with categories for Novice (seven to eight years old), Atom (nine to ten years old), Peewee (eleven to twelve to years old), and Bantam (thirteen to fourteen years old). In 2004 the tournament had only one youth division for children between the ages of nine and ten, but this change was not for lack of youth interest: 'you see Saturday, we started games at eight this morning, and all seniors are going to start at eleven. We couldn't squeeze another game in. I could have a division for Peewee, for Atom, Bantam, and Midget [fifteen to seventeen years old], but we don't have the ice' (personal interview with tournament organizer). Another modification was the removal of the adult recreation division, which was previously in place for adult men wishing to play hockey but without the seriousness or physical contact of the competitive division. I asked the tournament organizer about this change and he laughed, 'People don't like watching that type of hockey.' I initially interpreted his comment as being disparaging towards weaker players, which seemed to undermine the inclusivity of the event. But he said, the problem was not with the less skilled players, but rather with 'guys that can skate, can shoot. Why are these guys not playing senior hockey? They can skate through the whole team, but put them on a real hockey team and see if they can do that. That's the kinda stuff people don't like. So, we took out that recreational division.' In contrast, he said people don't mind watching the thirty-five plus division, which

---

small mats made of cloth or animal skin in front of them. The opponent attempts to correctly guess which mat conceals the hidden stone/bone. The players are accompanied by other individuals who chant and drum throughout the game. The games at the Brandon tournament lasted for hours, and spectators packed the room to watch.

3 Tatanka was a professional wrestler whose persona drew from his Native American ancestry. The wrestling was not specific to First Nations peoples, however; the other wrestlers were not of Aboriginal heritage.

they continued to offer because these were 'the guys who have paid their dues in hockey, and now they're playing in thirty-five and over. You know people don't mind watching that. You know these guys have played their heart out for their community, and now they are playing in the old-timer division, more finesse and stuff like that.' The tournament also offers a female[4] division, which increased by one team in 2004 with the inclusion of a team made up of players from the First Nations University of Canada.

The category with the highest skill and which garnered the most attention was the senior men's division. In previous years the tournament has been referred to as the Stanley Cup of First Nations hockey, attracting the best First Nations players and teams from across the country. It offered prize money totalling about $26,000 ($10,000 for first place, $8,000 for second, etc.). The prizes were reduced when the Dakota Ojibway Tribal Council moved the event to Winnipeg in 1999. Sioux Valley Dakota First Nation continued the tradition of holding a tournament in Brandon, but under the new name of the First Nation Winter Celebrations. Without the economic backing of the Dakota Ojibway Tribal Council, Sioux Valley Dakota First Nation needed to minimize financial risks in running the event and provide prize money that matched team registration dollars. In 2004 there were eighteen teams registered in the adult divisions, each paying registration fees of $800. Total registration fees added up to $14,400, which meant $14,400 would be paid out to various categories of winners (the majority went to the senior men's division: first place received $5,000; second place $2,500; third place $600; and fourth place $400). The tournament organizer explained that even for 'the teams that don't win, we give them something, like enough for

---

4 At this point it is important to state that I did not focus on female hockey or the manner in which it is situated against the dominant male version of the sport. For one, when I initially applied for funding for this research the proposed study was to examine *masculinity* in First Nations hockey. But once fieldwork began, the topic seemed far too specific and my general knowledge too limited to embark down this avenue. Instead I simply focused on male First Nations hockey in general. Secondly, the tournament format was highly condensed and it did not afford me the time to observe male hockey in its entirety. Adding the female divisions and working with female participants would simply not have been possible under such a research format. With this said, the female game is growing exponentially across the country and warrants studies dedicated to its development and the complexities that surround it.

gas money or something. It's a long trip here.' Offering over $14,000 in prize money may seem like an attractive feature for a recreational hockey tournament, but as we will see later, some tournaments offer prize money as high as $40,000. Tournament organizers were aware of the potential impact a reduction in prize money might cause, but with the tournament broadening its scope and becoming more of a winter festival, along with its prestigious history as one of the country's premier hockey tournaments, it was hoped that the event would continue to attract top-quality teams and players. In speaking to the players it was apparent that the tournament's status had diminished somewhat as a result of the reduced purse, but it continues to be one of the premier hockey tournaments in Canada. As witnessed in 2003 and 2004, the tournament continues to attract First Nations hockey players in the latter stages of their professional hockey careers, former professional players, and players with major junior or varsity hockey experience.

This notion of tournament prestige and honour, one of the critical features of the Brandon tournament, resonates in tournament play, with participants, and with players. When Don first told me about the tournament he said there 'was less money than previous years, but the intensity/prestige of the Brandon tourney remains.' What must be acknowledged here is that the tournament is a recreational event, despite the elite and recreational categories it contains. The players in the elite division have in almost every situation played at the highest levels of organized hockey, and in some cases are household names in Canada. Playing in a community hockey tournament would hardly seem to hold much significance to players of such high calibre, yet watching tournament play and seeing the players compete and celebrate wins so intensely I was convinced otherwise. During an interview with the tournament organizer, I asked him about an issue pertaining to teams who have the resources to 'buy' players rather than using players from their own community, and if this caused any resentment for teams not able or willing to use players outside of their community. The organizer evaded the question entirely, speaking to the tournament's importance to communities and players, which somehow made costs of buying players not only acceptable, but rather a reflection of the tournament's value:

That happened a few years ago, the last year that we had that last $10,000 payout. We had a team from Swift Lake, and usually there were only two players from Swift Lake, the rest of them were all bought. They rented all their players. They spent $26,000. I mean it's just huge for our communities . . . It's been referred to – a few years ago, they did a documentary, Reggie Leach was here, TSN[5] was here, and it was like the Stanley Cup of [First Nations] hockey. So that's the way it was described. There's a lot of emotion involved when a team wins a tournament . . . And for this tournament, it's prestige. Like we just go for that big trophy; it's a huge trophy. The last team to have their names on it was the 2000 winners, because they didn't take it. All the other ones, they take the trophy with them, and they keep it. We just got it back the other day, yesterday, so we don't have time to engrave it or anything like that. And then tomorrow night, when we hand out that trophy again, whoever wins that trophy, they're going to want to take it home. And we'll get the same song and dance again, 'yeah we'll send it back.' But no, they'll keep it until next year. But I mean they earned it, they won it. And that's what this tournament is. There's a lot of prestige with this.

For those playing for their community, the importance of winning such a prestigious tournament is clear; yet the importance of the event for those not playing for their own community was perhaps even more interesting. In 2003 Don, who is originally from the Garden River Reserve in Ontario and who now lives in a major urban centre in Canada, won the event playing for Sandy Bay, a tiny reserve in Manitoba. The team was composed of amazing local and national talent, with one of the players having played a short stint with the Vancouver Canucks and their goaltender currently on contract with a professional Division I hockey team in Germany. After Don's team ended up winning the tournament, I went on the ice to snap team photographs and was asked to come back to the dressing room and celebrate with them. When I arrived in the dressing room, I was amazed at this assemblage of current and former professional hockey players, clearly elated after winning the event. I wrote in my field notes:

The other thing to note was the incredible jubilation seen after winning the game. It was as if this was the Stanley Cup. The players mauled one another. In the dressing room after the game, the players looked simply exhausted. Almost all of them were smoking cigarettes. The room was blue with smoke, there was chatter, and there was an exhausted satisfaction. One of the star players yelled at one point, 'See what happens

---

5 TSN is one of Canada's sport television networks, owned by Bell Media Inc.

when we don't drink on Saturdays boys!!' But other than that, there were few shouts. The room beamed with pride and satisfaction. It was a really special experience.

Both the 2003 and 2004 events were well attended. The seating capacity for the main ice surface at the Keystone Centre Complex is 5,008 plus standing room. For the final games on Sunday, roughly half of the seats were filled, meaning that they were attracting over 2,000 fans to watch the final games. In addition to spectators watching hockey, people filled the complex for events like the pow wow, bingo, or the craft show that extended throughout the complex. The costs of running an event such as this are significant. The tournament organizer explained that it was $50,000 just to rent the complex for the three days. The tournament committee hoped to at least break even, but also to make some profit which would go in part to covering tournament costs for the following year and also be redirected into youth sport programming for the Sioux Valley Dakota First Nation. Over the course of the weekend I attended some of the festival's other (non-hockey) events and noted that each event was well attended with males and females of all different ages. The audience was predominantly First Nation, but there were non-First Nations peoples present as well. The festival was well organized and of professional quality in its management and operations. The whole experience was positive, which was what the tournament organizer said was his intention in putting it on and why he has continued to be involved for the past two decades:

It's a lot of fun. I went from playing in this tournament to volunteering at this tournament. I kinda worked my way through, from being a timekeeper to running the whole event. To be here this long and meeting the same people over and over all these years and they're so happy about this event. To them it's a lot of fun. And for me, it's going to sound sappy, but that's rewarding to me to see someone saying, this is great, it's great fun. Kids playing minor hockey, kids at the pow wow, kids at the square dance, just kids having a blast, you know. Grandfathers watching their grandkids now. That grandfather, back in the 70s, was playing in this tournament. There's lots of tradition here.

Kenora

The Winter Tribal Days event was my first experience conducting research at a First Nations hockey tournament, and from this I expected subsequent tournaments to resemble what I had observed in Brandon. The next open tournament I attended was the North American First Nations Winterfest Tournament of Champions, an event that occurs annually on Easter weekend in Kenora, Ontario. Kenora is a town of approximately 15,000 people, and is located in a relatively remote area of northwestern Ontario, less than sixty kilometres from the Manitoba border. As is to be expected in a small and isolated community, the facility options in Kenora were significantly limited in comparison to those available in Brandon. Without a multipurpose venue like the Keystone Complex, the tournament was housed in two separate arenas about ten kilometres apart. The central site for the tournament was the Kenora Recreation Centre Ice Skating Rink, which has one rink pad, seating for approximately 2,000 spectators, and a small lobby area with snack bar services. The alternate site was in a formerly separate community called Keewatin, which amalgamated with Kenora in 2000. Keewatin is another small community and has an even smaller, more basic arena than Kenora's. Seating in the facility consisted of only a few rows of benches on one side of the rink, which limited the tournament organizers' ability to attract spectators and important gate receipts. From the outset it was apparent that this tournament offered a much different experience than that which took place in Brandon, in large part because of the limited infrastructure.

The North American First Nations Hockey Tournament was exactly what the name stated: a hockey tournament. Unlike the festival-type event offered in Brandon, all activities at the Kenora event centred on adult male hockey. Also unlike the Brandon tournament, there was only one division, made up of twenty-four teams. The initial games served as a type of relegation round where teams either won and moved on to the A-side championship, or lost and were relegated down to the B-side championship. These brackets were neatly identified in the tournament program as the 'Winners' and the 'Losers.' The first-place prize money for the A side was $10,000 and second-place was $5,000. On the B side, first-place teams received $2,000, and second-place received $1,000. The reference to North America in the tournament title is misleading, as the teams either came from northwestern Ontario or Manitoba. However, since this was an open tournament, where players were not restricted to play for their home community, the event attracted players from all across the country. The team Don played for represented a remote fly-in community from northwestern Ontario, but only one player was from the actual community. The rest of the players came from British Columbia, Alberta, Saskatchewan, and Ontario. The tournament was advertised as recreational rather than senior, meaning that it was a non-bodychecking event. This was also different from Brandon. In speaking with the tournament organizer and players, I learned that the recreational format makes the tournament more inclusive; players who are not comfortable playing bodychecking hockey are still able to participate. For many of the players who come from remote communities, there is no such thing as organized hockey and they have not had the opportunity to play formal bodychecking hockey. Without learning how to give and receive bodychecks they are not only disadvantaged, but also vulnerable to serious injury. The tournament has therefore been transformed in recent years from a bodychecking to a non-bodychecking event. What the tournament organizer did not state in our formal interview, but which was also a factor in the decision to offer a non-bodychecking tournament, was the significant cost associated with insuring body-contact tournaments. The tournament organizer in Brandon spoke of this in our interview. By offering a recreational event, the tournament was not a registered hockey tournament and avoided the insurance costs associated with such status. As a result, there was a greater range of talent from player to player and from team to team, in contrast to the parity seen in Brandon.

It is worthwhile to focus briefly on the discrepancy in skill level, because it speaks to underlying tensions that are at times present in tournaments such as these. In speaking to Don about the Kenora tournament, he explained that there were likely four to six 'money teams,' which meant that there were four to six teams made up of players who were being compensated for playing on a particular team. These four to six teams would likely be the only serious contenders for the championship, as the rest of the teams were made up of players from their own communities. As a result many of the games were grossly lopsided, with teams losing by seven or eight goals after the first period of play. Early in the event I recorded that there were players who appeared to have little hockey experience yet were playing next to guys who at one point played professional hockey. In the margins of my field book I wrote: *It's a good thing this tournament is not body contact, otherwise these guys would get killed.* At the same time, these community-based teams and their fans did not appear to be overly concerned by their superior opponents and approached the game with a certain lightheartedness and joviality. Near the conclusion of one game where a team was losing 8–0, the losing team scored with only a few minutes remaining. The fans, made up of local community members, let out a huge cheer as though a goal against this strong team was a victory unto itself. This was their second game and second lopsided loss, and as a result of the loss they were out of the tournament. At the conclusion of the game the players got together on the ice and posed in a celebratory photo shoot with various community/family members snapping souvenir photos. They were happy for simply putting a team together and participating in the event, which was mutually shared with family and friends who had travelled a significant distance (and paid considerable money) to watch and support them over the two days.

The stark contrast between elite talent and limited skill at the Kenora tournament led to humorous scenes unlike anything I had seen in Brandon; these displays were more reminiscent of the informal hockey I had observed among the Esketemc First Nation. Over the course of the tournament I made various observations about the contrasting appearance and play of some players and teams compared to the highly serious teams: one team did not have matching jerseys; players were often seen playing with smiles on their faces; many of the players were out of shape and clearly had not played hockey for some time; and on multiple occasions teams showed up without goalies for the first part of the game, but in one situation the team that had the goalie was not able to take advantage and score on the empty net, eventually losing the game. Sitting in the stands I overheard a conversation between two players who had already played and were now watching the game. I recorded their exchange in my field notes: *'I tried running a week before the tournament but hurt myself and had to stop.' His friend then said, 'Our team had a practice last week but no one could finish the skating drills.' Both guys laughed.* In contrast to this were the more serious teams paying players and even coaches (most often not of First Nations background) to be part of their team. In an interview I conducted with one individual who personally financed one of the teams, he said that he paid over $10,000 to put his team together. At the conclusion of the tournament I saw envelopes of money being passed to the coach and to certain players. It was explained to me that if the team had won the tournament, certain players would receive $500. This amount would be over and above money they received for air travel, food, and hotel lodging to come to the event. This team lost in the championship, so instead of $500, players only received $250.

The investment some people were willing to make to win the tournament was evident on the ice, where players were seen striving and sometimes fighting to win. It is difficult to relay here how intense the games could be, but there is one defining feature, which is not exclusive to First Nations hockey but was a fixture at all of the events I attended and captured what was at stake: the overtime format. Overtime is a necessary component to any type of elimination sporting event, in that elimination games cannot conclude in a tie. In hockey there are a variety of overtime formats, but most involve some form of extended game play and then perhaps a round of penalty shots. In North American professional hockey, the penalty shot format is reserved only for regular season play; for playoff overtime, game play is extended in a sudden death format, where the first team that scores wins. The games may take hours to complete, but from a North American perspective, it is the only legitimate manner in which to determine a winner. Professional hockey playoffs, however, are not limited to a single weekend and do not face time restrictions. Since most First Nations tournaments occur over a weekend, it is imperative to have timely resolutions to the games. To this end, a creative overtime format has been devised. If the score is still tied after regulation play, the teams play sudden overtime segments that start with five-on-five play (plus one goalie in each net) for one minute. If a goal is not scored, each team removes one skater, and they play for another minute four on four. They will continue to remove skaters from the ice until there is only one skater per side (plus the goalies). If there is still no winner, the game moves to a series of penalty shots. There can be slight variations to the rules. In Kenora, the players are able to make shift changes during the overtime. In Brandon, however, teams can only use the players who started the five on five shootout; there are no substitutions. This means that one of the players will remain on the ice for the entire five minutes of overtime, or until the other team scores. This is essentially a five minute shift, which in hockey terms is unheard of. In either case though, the players are seriously fatigued by the end of regulation and this overtime format is absolutely gruelling – especially considering that the players are competing in up to five or six games over the course of three days. By the time the overtime gets to two on two, the four skaters are exhausted. If it moves to one on one – something I witnessed on three different occasions over the two years of watching tournament hockey – the players are completely drained and typically go into a defensive mode where they simply do not want to give up a scoring opportunity.

In the first year I attended the Kenora tournament, two games went into overtime; in the second year I witnessed only one. Each occasion generated pandemonium in the stands and frenzied action on the ice. In my field notes I recorded one especially entertaining overtime session:

The game was amazing. It went down to a one-on-one overtime. With no time on the clock, the other team scored. Incredible scenarios of one on two, with the lone guy dominating play. Two-on-one chances with no scoring. The game was also filled with amazing talent and amazing plays. It was incredible to watch. I was literally on the edge of my seat. A penalty was called in the overtime so that the three on three turned into a three on two. X team failed to score though. When it dropped to two on one for X team, an X-team player got a penalty. It then went to one on one, but X team was supposed to be a player short: the question was, do they play one on zero, or two on one. The organizers had not encountered this before and did not know what to do with the situation: there was no official rule to say. The refs and tournament organizers consulted for a while and after five minutes worked out this solution: X team could either play zero on one or one on two. They obviously decided to play one on two. Despite the odds, their defenceman was dominating the Y-team players. X team made a change and player J almost scored one on two. But by not scoring and then trying again to score, he got greedy, lost the puck, and gave up a breakaway with six seconds left. Y-team guy went up ice and scored on the buzzer. There was again controversy about whether the puck went in before the buzzer. The game was amazing, but in losing, X team collapsed.

In this particular game, there were three players from X team who had professional hockey experience and all competed to the best of their ability. The last player on the ice, who nearly scored but ended up giving up the breakaway on the final goal, was the most remarkable player I had encountered over the course of my fieldwork. He is one of three brothers (all exceptional in their own way) who made stunning plays that mesmerized opposing players and fans. He had the ability to stop on a dime, shift, and move in the opposite direction, completely outmaneuvering those around him. On a breakaway I witnessed him shift the goalie completely out of his net and score on what was ultimately an empty net. He resembled NHL superstar Paval Datsyuk, yet was here playing his heart out to get his team to the next level. When the overtime goal went in, he and his teammates were furious, still not willing to concede defeat even after it was all over. This player had played junior hockey and had brief stints in semi-professional leagues, yet here in this small town of Kenora, playing for a team that he had no community affiliation with, he played with remarkable passion.

This exemplifies the contrasts characteristic of the Kenora tournament, where some players are seen agonizing to win and others are simply glad to be on the ice. It is also, as mentioned earlier, a source of tension for many players, fans, teams, and communities, in that this mercenary framework is creating stark divisions between teams with the resources to buy players and those who either do not have the resources or choose not to spend them on hockey players.

These tensions were more apparent in Kenora than in Brandon, because the organizer had gradually transformed the event from a senior tournament to a recreational, non-body-contact tournament. The organizer explained that when the tournament began in the late 1980s it was an elite event with only the best teams. He said that he now wanted the event to be more inclusive, and the recreational format made this possible. As a result, there were teams who were able to enter the tournament with limited playing experience and in some cases even little desire to seriously compete. These teams enter the tournament more for the social experience, which the organizer stated was one of its key purposes. He wanted this to be an opportunity for positive community interaction. For many people in this region of Ontario, it is an opportunity to leave the reserve, which has limited amenities, and visit a more urban centre. People are able to get important shopping done and also take advantage of eating out at restaurants and experiencing local nightlife. With twenty-four teams coming to town, along with a strong contingent of community supporters, a small town like Kenora is overwhelmed with visitors and bustles throughout the entire weekend.

There are other teams, however, who enter the tournament with the intention of competing, but are unable to compete at the same level as the more elite tournament teams because of the limited formal hockey opportunities available in remote areas. Because there is only one division and all teams compete against one another, on more than one occasion serious conflict ensued. Two separate brawls broke out during the tournament, starting on the ice and then extending into the stands. On one occasion the local police were called to break up the altercation. I did not witness the actual brawl because I was on my way back from the Keewatin arena to see a game at the Kenora rink. As I approached the parking lot I could see five police cruisers parked outside the front entrance and dozens of people milling about buzzing with excitement. When I arrived people proceeded to tell me about what had happened. They explained that a fight broke out on the ice that then carried into the stands and into the dressing room hallways. They said that one team made up of adolescent players was getting picked on by the other team which was made up of adults – the typical age for this event. Family members of the junior team began taking exception to their younger kids getting hurt, and when a fight broke out on the ice, the fans got involved. When I went into the arena I interviewed the security guard about it, and he said that the fight began on the ice, turned into a line brawl, extended into one of the teams' benches and then carried on into the stands. Punches were flying and even innocent people were getting hurt. A woman eventually called 911. Once the brawl extended into the stands the referees refrained from getting involved, leaving ill-equipped security guards to try and break up the melee. The game was cancelled but neither team was thrown out of the tournament. I ended up visiting with the junior team and their families the following day, which I summarized in my field notes as follows:

I was sitting with community members from the team that brawled yesterday and ended up speaking with them. There were two men in front of me, both huge guys. The one on my left had a badly bruised and swollen face from the fight. I asked them to talk about what happened and they said the older team picked on and fought their young team. Their team is made up of young players who look like they're all around eighteen or younger. They all wear full face shields and the fact that they're called the juniors suggests that this is a youth team competing in the men's tournament. I spoke with the bruised-face guy and the woman with him after the game and I asked them about the role the cops played. They said the cops didn't do anything. The big guy in front of me jumped in and said, 'Yeah, cops don't get involved; they just sit outside while Natives beat the shit out of themselves.'

The violence that erupted speaks volumes about the strong ties community members feel towards one another and the great lengths to which they will go to stand up for one another, but it also speaks to the tensions that emerge as a result of two levels of play/experience colliding with one another.

During my interview with the tournament organizer he explained to me that one of the main reasons he started the tournament was to develop youth hockey. I found his comment odd considering that this was an adult hockey tournament. He said by watching the adults play, the youth would have greater incentive to get involved in the sport, which he said was working because of all the juniors involved in this year's event. At the same time, the event still maintains its legacy of being one of the premier hockey tournaments with considerable prize money available to the winners. As a premier event there is considerable prestige in winning it, which for some teams means buying the best possible players and even coaches to win the championship. It has created a type of bidding war for players, and players ultimately play for the team that offers them the most money. The stakes get higher as more money is spent on attracting the top players, yet this is all taking place within the new recreational, inclusive model. The contrasting levels of play provide humour and entertainment for some, but resentment for others whose players are not seen as having a fair chance to compete. And in some extreme cases like the example above, there is a perception that the disadvantaged players are being put at unnecessary risk of injury. While the violence of this particular event was atypical of tournament play, other participants expressed their discontent towards the persistence of mercenary tactics that they felt undermined community allegiance and the potential benefits of tournament play. In one conversation I had with a coach who had put together a team of younger players from his community, he explained that his team was 'a real community team' and felt players who only played for money missed the whole point of the tournament. He said two of his better players were lured away from playing on their team at the last minute because they were offered money to play for another team. One of them was their goaltender. Not surprisingly, their team was beat soundly throughout the tournament – in one game by eight goals. The tensions evident at the Kenora tournament point to larger issues about First Nations hockey and its evolution within the larger colonial imaginary. Here we have the distinctiveness of local community hockey in conflict with the professionalized model of sport based on performance and material gain. Yet as we move on to the next tournament in Prince George, British Columbia, the looming threat of the professionalized model of sport does not point to the erasure of First Nations hockey character and distinctiveness, but rather exacerbates it.

Prince George

The Prince George Lumber Kings tournament was the last event I would attend each tournament season. I was not initially planning to observe this tournament because I had already attended the events I had budgeted for in the first season. Don convinced me that of all the tournaments, I needed to see this one as it was the most entertaining of the circuit. The tournament takes place over a three-day period in mid-April. Prince George is a city of approximately 71,000 people, located in central British Columbia. Being a larger centre with multiple arenas, the city gives tournament organizers plenty of options for where to host the event. The main tournament setting was a dual-rink complex that housed one larger ice surface with significant capacity (likely 2,500 seats) and a smaller ice surface with seating limited to a couple of benches along one side of the rink. Between the two ice surfaces was a large lobby encased in windows so that people could watch games on either side. The lobby area also had small displays for local entrepreneurs to sell merchandise and crafts, and there was a canteen offering hot meals and snacks. All of the tournaments I attended were dry (non-alcoholic) events, but in previous years this lobby had once served as a bar area where spectators could drink and watch the games through the windows.

The Lumber Kings tournament has been running since 1984, and like the event in Brandon, has a reputation for being one of the best hockey tournaments in the country, attracting the best First Nations players. Both years I attended the tournament there were more current and former professional hockey players than at any other event I attended. Unlike at Brandon, the former professional players here were not ones who had marginal professional careers; they were outstanding players who were First Nations hockey celebrities. There were forty-one teams in total playing in multiple divisions. There was also a division for women's hockey for the first time in the tournament's history. When I arrived I was introduced to the tournament organizer and founder, Harley Chingee, who provided me with information about the tournament format and the various categories. After my first meeting with Harley I knew that this tournament was not like any of the others I had attended. To begin with, when Harley was going through the various categories with me, I noticed that the top division was listed as the B division. I asked him why there wasn't an A division and he responded, 'Oh, that's because in school a B is a Native A.' At first I did not understand what he meant, but as he started grinning, I caught on that he was making a joke about Aboriginal academic performance. He was intimating that First Nations kids weren't expected to get As. For them, getting a B was like getting an A for everyone else. When I first met Harley, it was outside of the main entrance and he was standing in front of a sign, which read, DUE TO THE RECENT EVENTS OF 9/11 SECURITY WILL CHECK ALL BAGS FOR OFFENSIVE WEAPONS. WILLIE THE BOMB SNIFFING DOG WILL CHECK ALL MOCCASINS FOR EXPLOSIVES.

More telling, however, was Harley's overview of the tournament, which he described as being tiered in terms of overall skill, but not in terms of competitiveness. All categories, except for the women's hockey, were bodychecking. He said the C and D divisions were often more competitive and more entertaining because of the fierce community rivalries, and that for some, 'it's just about seeing who's the toughest reserve.' He said players playing in the lowest division have never really played anywhere else, so when they play in this tournament it is like playing for the Stanley Cup. He said games get 'wild' and often end up in brawls (which I did witness on one occasion), or do not even finish at all. There were no reservations in the manner in which he provided this information, which was in contrast to all the other tournament organizers, who stressed positive elements of the events and would quickly downplay any of the negative associations with tournaments such as excessive drinking and violence. For Harley, the excessiveness of the event seemed to be its signature, or at least part of its aura; it is not something he apologizes for. At one point he told me that he schedules games between reserves that have the greatest rivalries to make sure the games are as intense as possible. He said that 'last year there was a game where the brawl on the ice extended into the stands' and so he scheduled them to face off against each other for their first game that afternoon. I made sure to attend the game, which lived up to the expectations:

The game was vicious; lots of hits and a fight took place. During the fight, the players were going ballistic right in front of their bench. One player had his stick cocked, ready to two-hand one of the fighters. The woman beside me was trying to calm the players down. She told us that last time these guys played, they didn't make it through the first period. How a brawl didn't ensue in this game was unknown to me.

What was clear was that this tournament had a type of edginess the others didn't, which made it a unique event. This tournament, which Harley had been running for the past nineteen years, seemed to reflect his wry sense of humour and general eccentricity. His status in the area is legendary, which was made known to me in a variety of ways, but perhaps best through the endless storytelling sessions that are integral to the hockey tournament experience.

Before going into greater detail about the tournament itself, it is important to describe some of these stories and their performative settings. These storytelling sessions provide the context needed to begin to understand some of the more extreme behaviours observed at the Prince George tournament. It needs stating that there was no pretence about this tournament. It was a hockey tournament. It possessed many of the same institutional problems systemic to the sport in general; that is, excessive drinking and violence. In the context of hockey, however, these extreme behaviours are a source of humour and are celebrated through hyperbolic retellings, often over drinks at a bar. Seeing the tournament through these stories helps to see it for what it is. The excessiveness of the tournament is one of the main reasons the players keep coming back, and I am sure it is why Don wanted me to attend this event.

SESSION ONE

As stated earlier, this was the last event I attended in the tournament year, and by this time I had built relationships with many of the players who were part of the tournament circuit. Unlike the earlier tournaments, where it took longer to build rapport with people, I felt comfortable enough on the first night to hang out with guys at the bar after their first game. Don's team had just finished blowing out a weaker opponent, where they not only hammered them on the scoreboard, but physically pounded them as well. After the game the guys returned to the hotel bar to get some food and have a few drinks. The tournament organizer, Harley, who managed and sponsored Don's team (the Prince George Lumber Kings), also joined the gathering. Three or four tables were pulled together so everyone could sit and listen to the stories featuring Harley or the tournament – both of which reflected on his character. The stories were collective performances, where guys would contribute a line or two resuming from where the last guy left off. They were typically short, but had multiple punch lines that were met with raucous laughter followed by more punch lines. On this particular night, the stories began with humorous anecdotes about Harley as coach of the Lumber Kings team and his vicious tirades on the bench. When players didn't perform as he expected he would scream at them on the ice, referring to one player as a 'fucking welfare bum' and another as a 'fucking midget.' His maniacal approach to coaching apparently paled, however, in comparison to his notorious stints as a tournament referee. In one story they talked about how the C and D divisions were so violent that it was getting increasingly difficult to get anyone to officiate the games. Eventually Harley had to ref some of the games himself, which proved even more problematic. Don recounted one story of Harley's officiating, which involved a player cross-checking another player to the head. Impersonating Harley, Don stood up and waved out his arms and said, 'No foul!' Apparently the guy responded with a wild two-handed swing of his stick towards the other guy, and again, 'No foul!' Don then said that the incident escalated into a brawl that got so bad that Harley just left the ice to let the players settle it themselves. They had to turn off the lights in the arena to restore order. Don performed the story with each incident becomingly increasingly egregious, which was met with escalated laughter to the point that the final episode had guys completely keeled over crying with laugher.

Don was one of the more skilful storytellers, and as the sessions went on he typically took centre stage. On this night the stories eventually moved away from Harley and began focusing on memorable First Nations tournament moments. Much of the humour centred on the distinctiveness of the tournaments, which played with stereotypes of First Nations hockey as being violent, scary, and unorganized. I attempted to capture some of the story details when I returned to my room later that night. Below is a brief excerpt from my notes:

A few years back Don was playing in this one tournament and there was a guy from one of the teams who had just gotten out of jail. In the warm-up he came on the ice with an Oka[6] bandana and a knife taped to the blade of his stick. The guys all laughed and contributed to the story by saying they were all shitting bricks at the time. Another tournament they were in was described as 'a shitty tournament with only five hundred bucks for prize money.' The story was about all the organizers cheating and making up the rules as the tournament went on. In the one game the organizer told them three of their players were suspended for the championship game for some rule that wasn't being enforced the whole tournament. The tournament guy said, 'Yes it [the rule] has been enforced,' and showed him the rules. It turns out the rules were for the girls' division and totally didn't apply to them. This account was followed by more laughter. Don continued with

---

6 The reference here is to the 1990 Oka crisis, a land dispute that resulted in armed conflict between the Kanesatake First Nation and local police and, later, military authorities. The conflict involved Mohawk warriors engaging in armed standoffs with Canadian soldiers. Media images of Mohawk men and women going face-to-face with the Canadian military inspired even greater respect and fear for this group, which already had a reputation for being fearless warriors.

more bullshit about the inconsistent application of rules to help the local team win. He then came back saying, 'The guy kept pointing to the rule book, look at the small print! Rules are subject to change at any time.' More laughter. Donny punctuated all this with, 'Yeah, and the rulebook was written in French.'

SESSION TWO

The last night of the tournament proved to be an even richer storytelling session than the first night. The Lumber Kings had won the B-side championship and the guys were celebrating their victory, but also the fact that the players had one last night together before disbanding again and returning to whatever parts of Canada they came from. In an interview I conducted with Don earlier that year he explained why he loved playing in these tournaments. He said:

> I love hockey tournaments because it's a microcosm of a whole season in one weekend. And so really it's a short season in one weekend, and it's success or failure. Once it's over, it's bang, that's it, it's over, like a little season is done. You can't ever go back and win Brandon 2003 which is over, and that's for me personally what I try to get across to guys especially when we come close to losing the big money games. Fuck guys we're here now man, this is why we're here, the games that are played in tournaments, let's not waste them, let's not be happy with just the final game in Brandon, and shit let's go out as winners. You know and then obviously that's how you measure your success. You go there and win, and you know it's like a little mini season.

As I listened to the players share in this victory celebration on the final night, the significance of what Don had said became more apparent as players were now celebrating their victory but also saying goodbye to one another. The tone of the evening was very different than the first night, where guys were being reacquainted, excited with the prospects of what the weekend might bring. On this final night, after two very late nights and four hockey games, the guys were less exuberant, but content. The stories were more individual performances, unlike the collective banter of the first night. Guys sat back enjoying hearing stories they have heard many times before, but somehow get funnier with each retelling. The stories continued to focus on past tournament experiences and First Nations hockey distinctiveness, but again with a self-deprecatory style. Often the dark content, dealing with issues of extreme violence and racism, was naturalized in the narratives, which became a source of humour. One story, for example, dealt with a bar brawl that extended into the streets. The following account from my field notes aims to capture both the content of the story and the players' reactions.

The story involves a player named Harry who was making faces at a white guy while attempting to make a shot playing pool. Despite Donny's warning, he continued to do so until the white guy got pissed and a fight broke out. At this point in the story, the entire table is listening to Don's every word.

Donny says, 'I knew we were in trouble when Harry took out his front teeth and said, "Okay, let's go!"' The fight broke out with 'twenty white guys and twenty Indian guys going into the street.' Harry began kicking the shit out of the guy and in the process pulled the guy's shirt over his head and every-one noticed how hairy he was. While Harry was kneeling on the guy's chest, pounding him, he yelled, 'Who's Hairy now? Who's Hairy now?'

The guys break into hysterics even though some have heard the story before. Don continues once the laughter has died down. He says that while the brawl was going on, he was going around and picking up the guys' jackets and hold-ing them for them. With twenty jackets over his arm he was incapacitated and couldn't pair up with anyone in the brawl. At this point in the story, he jokes by saying, 'Hey, I can't fight' and motions to imaginary jackets over his arm. Guys are laughing at his 'contribution' to the brawl.

Don continues that during the brawl one of his own guys said, 'Hey, help out!' Don said, 'I can't, man, I got a Nike jacket in here.' The guys at the table are dying with laughter. Don then concludes with, 'So every time there's a brawl I'm just hoping someone throws off their jacket.' There's more laughter. I too am in hysterics at this point.

The bar/street brawl is a semi-regular occurrence during this tour-nament weekend, which often results from tensions between First Nations and non-First Nations patrons. This story takes these racial tensions and produces a humorous narrative. But this is more than a funny story. The story is also an act of empowerment, with Harry not only beating up the 'white guy,' but making him the butt of his joke as well. Don's role as 'coat monitor' also cleverly situates him above the corporal battles around him, outwitting even his own teammates who were doing battle around him. The self-deprecatory style is suddenly turned on its head, as Don pokes fun at the lack of teeth, the name 'Harry,' the juvenile behaviour of making faces at others, and his own unwillingness to fight; yet it is Don and his teammates who in the end are able to say, 'Look who's laughing now, eh.'

The statement 'look who's laughing now' is critical not simply for this narrative, but for the entire tournament. In many ways the tournament operated like a private joke, in that if you were not privy to its context, you would not understand it. This is not a comment about the tournament organization or the play itself, which was as good if not better than any other tournament I attended. In fact the sponsorship for this event was tremendous, covering prize payouts and in some years much of the facility costs. What I am referring to is the underlying sense of humour that was only evident if someone clued you in. For example, in 2003 the tournament paid tribute to one of the Lumber Kings players who was apparently retiring from tournament hockey. In the *Prince George Citizen*, the city's major newspaper, half of a page in the sports section was dedicated to the 'D-man hanging up his Lumber Kings jersey' (Peters 2003, 10). The article focuses on the 'career' of Joe Prince, who '[a]fter 12 seasons of bodychecks and bruises on the native hockey circuit with the Prince George Lumber Kings . . . is ready to put his skates into storage' (ibid.). The article reads like a typical sports journalism piece covering the career of a professional hockey player. It pays tribute to his career, highlighted by his steady point production for the Lumber Kings, and culminating with his induction into the Hockey Hall of Fame in Saskatoon. As the article progresses, the focus shifts from accolades to Prince's gradual realization that his battle-worn body was no longer able to compete as it once did, leading him to endure in his last remaining years by playing with a more defensive style. The article came out on the Saturday of the tournament, informing people that there was going to be a ceremony honouring Joe before the Lumber Kings game, and providing publicity for the tournament. At the hotel bar the night before, however, I overhead Harley mentioning something about a newspaper tribute that was going to be released the next day, to which the guys all started laughing. It turns out the piece was a roast rather than a legitimate sports article, and was written to pay tribute to their friend and teammate Joe Prince, who in reality was a great guy, but not so great a hockey player. It's an inside joke though. If anyone read the piece without knowing Harley or the tournament's humorous traditions, one would likely assume the article was genuine. There are slight hints that more attentive readers might pick up, like teammate Joey Potskin poking fun at their twenty-eight-year-old friend, saying, 'The old body still goes – he throws the odd hit here and there when he can catch somebody'; or the fact that there is no such thing as the Hockey Hall of Fame in Saskatoon – there is a Sports Hall of Fame but there is no record of a Joe Prince being inducted in 2002 as referenced in the article, or in any other year. Those who are very familiar with the tournament would also have caught on to the fact that Harley tries to roast a player every year in some manner. In 2004 they poked fun at First Nation Circuit regular Corey Potskin in the tournament program. The opening lines read, '27 year old, Corey, is a veteran of the Lumber Kings! He started playing hockey on the "Hood" streets at age 3, with pampers on.' All of this forces us to look again at 'who's laughing now.' The tournament is a First Nations event attended predominantly by First Nations people and the joke is directed towards this audience. Those on the outside, such as the non-Aboriginal population of Prince George who write about these things in local newspapers, or people like myself researching the subject, could easily miss the element of humour.

I have attempted to demonstrate here the complexities of coming to know something when one is clearly positioned outside of the cultural fabric in which it is produced. Perhaps more importantly, I wish to stress the cultural specificities of what is being described, in that by conducting research on the tournaments it exposed how little I understood about First Nations hockey tournaments or about First Nations hockey in general. When I initially started this fieldwork I kept trying to 'see' what is distinctive about First Nations hockey, how it is different from what I understand hockey to be within a dominant Euro-Canadian framework. In formal interviews I would ask First Nations players to try to give me their thoughts on the distinctiveness of First Nations hockey, a question that players would politely try to respond to, but that was clearly not something they were concerned about. In fact, my question seemed irrelevant. What was taking place before me was First Nations hockey. It was played by First Nations people, for First Nations audiences. In Prince George I slowly started to get this, in large part because 'I didn't get it.' I was not part of the story, even though the guys would occasionally clue me in. I wish to make this evident as I begin describing the tournament itself and relaying various observations made over the course of these two weekends in 2003 and 2004.

The Lumber Kings tournament provided a dramatic range of skill across the multiple divisions. It is worthwhile mentioning that in 2004 the division names changed from 2003. Instead of the highest division being the B division, in 2004 it was the A division, followed by the L, D, C, and O divisions (rather than corresponding alphabetically, the division letters stood for All Speed Division, Ladies Division, Devils Division, Canucks Division, and Oldtimers Division). The games that attracted the most attention were the A- (or B- depending on the year) division games – people would come from all parts of western Canada to watch the star-laden teams play. In 2004 in particular, the First Nations hockey celebrities participating in the event drew significant crowds. The lower divisions also drew large crowds, but for different reasons; they were made up of community teams, and entire communities would come to support their players. I interviewed one long-time local community member who, as a child during the early years of the tournament, used to sneak in to watch the games. He is now actively involved in First Nations hockey and in organizing the Prince George tournament. He stated, 'For the A side, basically you have people in the stands who are picking their teams at that game. They're there to watch the good hockey. And from B down, they bring their fans, right? So they have a big following. It's their people at the arena. So let's say, I don't know, Canim Lake, for instance, they have their fans following their team. But the A division, they're simply fans of good hockey more than anything.' In addition, the lower divisions were highly competitive and entertaining to watch even as the skill level was reduced. Unlike the Brandon event where there was one major division and the remaining divisions more or less providing recreational opportunities for tournament goers, the Lumber Kings tournament had highly skilled and fiercely competitive players that filtered down into the lower divisions. Many of these players would have been able to play in the top divisions in any of the other tournaments, but were not recruited by any of the A-division teams; there is a two-tiered system in place where players are either recruited onto the sponsored teams and play in the top divisions, or have to play with their own local teams in the lower divisions.

The process is reminiscent of professional hockey drafting systems where players can only participate in the league if they are provided an opportunity (either through a draft or an invitation), although in this case players are completely unrestricted free agents and seasons only last one weekend. This process of recruitment has impacted the tournament so that local players who were once the stars are being replaced by all-stars from the across the country. The tournament participant/organizer previously mentioned saw it this way:

What I learnt, Mike, from year one to year twenty, was the last five or six years the A division turned out into an All-Star event. Like basically there was no limit on who they picked up. In year one, your ringer was from the next community type thing. It wasn't from like [laughs], from Ontario or Quebec. And just the amount of pro players playing in it over the last few years, I would say in the first eight years there were two divisions or like one division the first seven years. The eighth year it moved to two divisions, an A and a B concept, because on Sunday morning you were still having scores of 17–1 kind of thing. So it was moved to a two-tiered format. And then a third division was added. And then probably by the twelfth, thirteenth year, the guys who came to the first one were getting to be old-timers age. So they created the old-timers division.

I had been encountering this theme of transformation throughout the tournament season, which posed tensions for those striving to resist this type of tournament professionalization. I too was unsettled by what I was interpreting as the encroachment of a professional sport model on a more 'authentic' version of First Nations hockey, but by attending the Lumber Kings tournament, alternative readings were made available. For one, the proliferation of divisions did not devalue less-skilled community hockey. Instead, for many participants and fans it provided an enabling function, in that many of the players who came from smaller remote communities, and who do not have access to organized hockey, were able to participate in an event where they were able to shine. Don explained it to me as such: 'Many [of these players] would not be able to play in these tournaments because they were not good enough. For them, this tournament serves as their chance to shine, to be stars, to be the best. It may be B, C, or D, but they are champions nonetheless.' Don also said that the lower divisions provided a window into more local expressions of sport and local community practices that A players, who often live in large urban centres, enjoyed going to watch.

Over the course of both years at the Lumber Kings tournament, I attended many of the lower division games – at times with Don and his teammates. Harley would let us know in advance about games with intense community rivalries, which typically led to fights or even brawls. During these games the fans were often more involved than they were at the A-division games. In fact the fans at this tournament were more intense than those at any of the other tournaments I attended. Fans would hurl verbal abuse at what was deemed weak or cowardly behaviour. I noted on several occasions a type of fan interaction that was directed towards the ice but also aimed to draw a reaction from surrounding fans. At one point I wrote:

This is tough hockey; fans cheer the violence, they participate in the violence.
The fans have been screaming at the games with the same intensity of the play-
ers, calling for more violence:
'Start hitting!'
'Kill him!' yells one lady.
'Get that fucking fag!'

At one game, an episode transpired as follows:

We're watching a game that has been two hours of brutal hitting, stick work,
and a couple of fights. People are yelling profanities towards the ice. Player
offers mock masturbation gesture towards mocking fans. A player went down
to injury because of getting attacked from behind with a crosscheck. It looked
like he was seriously hurt, but he continued to play and only went down later.
Fans screamed, calling him a 'faker,' a 'pussy,' and saying he should be kicked
out. One man yells at the ref, 'Fucking call it you blind bastard!' Blue team
fans yell 'Go blue go!' White team fans join in unison but insert 'home' at the
conclusion of each cheer: 'Go blue go home!'

The fan interaction was not always hostile. At times the derogatory
comments had an entertaining function, making other fans laugh:

I attended a B-side game this morning and some comments need to be made.
Some people were cheering very loudly. The comments were derogatory, loud,
and violent, but they provided humour. One guy in particular was the loudest.
Everything he said ended with, 'you cocksucker!'

The lower division games had a carnivalesque air about them, not
simply because of the unruly, vulgar, and derisive behaviours, but because of the collective manner in which they were experienced. The
action in the stands bled into what was taking place on the ice, and vice
versa. Fans won and lost with their teams. On the rare occasions that violence escalated on the ice, fans were there ready to defend the players
in whatever way possible. In Kenora I interpreted the fans' intervention in the on-ice brawl to stem from tensions associated with the stark
discrepancies in skills and resources among players and teams. What
this interpretation does not acknowledge, however, is the enduring
significance of community teams; rather than being subsumed by the
mercenary team models, community teams in fact thrive as meaningful
expressions of the community. I will speak more to this when discuss-

ing the community-modelled tournaments, but it is important to state here how the value of local expressions of sport is exposed when playing within an elite tournament framework. Against the star-studded A-division, the local teams appear more meaningful and are a vital part of the Lumber Kings tournament experience. The A division, however, provides a much different experience and enables a whole new set of meanings.

Before providing details about A-division tournament play, it is useful to relay part of a conversation I had with Don about the direction in which First Nations tournaments are heading. I asked Don if he thought the current model is somehow unfair to smaller communities who are unable to afford to 'buy' players, or if these 'bought' teams somehow undermine the importance of the tournaments. Matter-of-factly, Don responded, 'Mike, what would you do? Play for free or play for a team that will pay you to play?' His response pointed to my own limited understanding of the tournaments and the players themselves. The players who were now being recruited from across the country and paid to play for the weekend were not just elite First Nations hockey players, but some of the best players in the country. As professional, major junior, or varsity players, they competed with players from around the world. They were already exposed to the highly commodified world of elite hockey where players are drafted, traded, sold, and bought. The fact that this is now occurring in First Nations hockey is not perceived as a disservice, then, but rather a testament to how far it has come. In another interview, Don was quick to point out that in 'white tournaments, there is no money, like you pay say three hundred bucks for your team to enter, and if you win the tournament you get four hundred bucks back for the team . . . The thrill of winning is still there, but there's no monetary incentive.' The tournaments are showcases of First Nations hockey excellence, and for Don the money involved is simply a reflection of the high calibre of players that are participating.

It is this notion of showcasing First Nations excellence that makes A-division hockey such an important site for cultural enunciation. People came together at the Lumber Kings tournament to witness the incredible talent of both senior and more junior players. When I returned to the tournament for the second time, I was surprised to find out that recently retired NHL enforcer Gino Odjick was going to play. Word that he was playing created a tremendous buzz, and First Nations and non-First Nations people alike filled the arena to see him. This, according to one of the tournament participants, was not unique; the A division drew this type of crowd every year because the hockey is that good:

> There were even non-native people from Prince George that approached me and were quite disappointed that it didn't go on last year[7] because they looked forward to seeing this brand of hockey. We have the Junior A and the WHL here, but a lot of the Prince George guys, a lot of them are local and they did play on the Spruce Kings, so a lot of the non-native fans would come. For instance when the *Citizen* wrote that the Lumber Kings would be using Spruce Kings players, a lot of the Spruce Kings fans came out for that reason.

People also jammed the rink to see younger players who were currently playing major junior hockey in Canada and who were now NHL prospects. I met one person who was from the Kainai First Nation in southern Alberta. He drove fifteen hours to watch his son play. His son had just finished his last season playing with the Lethbridge Hurricanes of the Western Hockey League. I recorded our conversation in my field notes as follows:

> *His son played for the Lethbridge Hurricanes and he was now pursuing a pro career. So his dad had many opportunities to see him play amazing hockey, but still wanted to leave his ranch and make the fifteen hour drive to see his son play in this hockey tournament. This speaks to the significance of the tournaments – they have real value and people make sacrifices to come.*

Most people who came, however, had no direct affiliation with the teams or players on the ice. For some it was an opportunity to visit with friends and family who they rarely had the chance to see. One Elder told me that 'I see most of these people once a year' and that the tournament was 'a great opportunity for community gathering.'

Despite the large number of fans at the A-side games, the atmosphere was not nearly as intense as the lower divisions. People were vocal, cheering, criticizing, or making entertaining comments for the benefit of players and fans, but their comments were not unlike what you would hear at a professional or junior game. The Lumber Kings won

---

7 The tournament was not held in 2005 because of a variety of organizational challenges, but has since resumed.

the tournament the first year I was there, but lost in the finals in the second year. The games were hard fought and remarkable displays of skill, but had little impact on the crowd in terms of who won or lost. The players, too, were not overly emotional in victory or defeat. Both teams lined up and shook hands with one another after the game; it was evident that many of the players knew each other. After the games people lined up for a chance to get certain players' autographs or meet and talk to them. In almost all appearances the game was highly reminiscent of any elite-level hockey game I had attended in Canada. But two episodes reminded me that I was not at any other tournament – not even any other First Nations tournament. This was the Lumber Kings tournament, where the unexpected is always to be expected.

The first episode occurred at the end of the tournament in my first year of fieldwork, during the championship game. Three non-First Nations guys entered the arena and were visibly intoxicated. The men appeared to be in their mid-twenties and were cheering for some of their friends who were playing for the Prince George Lumber Kings. Throughout the game they shouted towards the ice, trying to get the attention of the players. Their drunken behaviour was starting to cause a scene and people in the stands were clearly displeased by their presence. Towards the end of the game, one of the men went to the other side of the rink and approached the Lumber Kings players' bench. The players were waving him to go away but in his drunken state he would not be reasoned with. The other two men, who had remained in the stands, were in hysterics watching their drunken friend attempt to get access to the players. The game finally ended with Prince George easily winning the championship. As both teams came out onto the ice and lined up to receive their trophies and prize money, the guy who had been hanging around the bench ran out onto the ice. The entire arena watched stunned as he dropped his pants and then dove as if into water. While his naked body slid across the ice, the tournament organizer stood by making formal award presentations over the loudspeaker, completely unfazed by the drunken display. There was some laughter, but mostly derisive comments from the audience. As I was watching the blond-haired Caucasian man try to get up from the ice with his pants around his ankles, reaching up as if he were climbing some imaginary rope suspended from the ceiling, all I could think of was the line from Don's story: 'Look who's laughing now.'

The second episode was less carnivaleque but equally rich in its destabilizing outcome. It occurred in the second year during a semifinal game between a reserve community from northern Alberta and the local Prince George Lumber Kings. The Alberta team was stacked with high-priced professionals and professional prospects, costing in the area of $20,000 to put together. With its star-studded lineup, this team was the clear favourite to win the tournament and also the main attendance draw. One of the biggest attractions was Gino Odjick, who over a ten-year NHL career was a fan favourite in every city he played – Montreal, Vancouver, New York, and Philadelphia. His reputation as a fearless combatant willing to fight any opponent, as well as being of First Nations ancestry, made him a hero amongst Aboriginal peoples in Canada and amongst many Canadian hockey fans in general. I use the word Aboriginal here deliberately because in many cases, Aboriginal success, whether First Nation, Inuit, or Métis, means success for all. While watching hockey on television in a remote First Nation community in northwestern Ontario, the family I was with wanted to watch an NHL game between the Nashville Predators and the St. Louis Blues. The family had a satellite dish with an NHL Centre Ice package, which allowed them to watch any game on the schedule on any particular day. At the time, Nashville and St. Louis were amongst the weaker and less popular teams in the league, but the family wanted to watch the game because Jordin Tootoo, an Inuk player from Nunavut, was playing for the Nashville Predators. Similarly, at the First Nation Winter Celebrations in Brandon, Manitoba, Jordin Tootoo was invited to drop the puck for the opening ceremonies of the championship game. When Jordin entered the arena, the fans went into a frenzy to get a chance to see him – at first I thought there was a brawl in the stands because of the tremendous commotion. Jordin Tootoo is a hero amongst First Nations peoples because of a shared indigenous heritage and a sense of Aboriginal collective identity.

Gino Odjick was from a First Nation in Quebec. During his NHL career he played multiple seasons for the Vancouver Canucks and as a result had a tremendous following in British Columbia and much of western Canada. In this northern British Columbia town, he was an obvious fan favourite and people buzzed in anticipation of seeing this hockey legend play before them in the relatively small Prince George rink. When my student and I were leaving that morning to go to the arena, we saw Gino in our hotel lobby surrounded by people wishing to get his autograph or a picture of him. People chanted his name during the game and many brought signs paying homage to him. As a hockey fan, I too was excited to watch him play and wondered how he would handle himself on the ice in a tournament like this. I was especially curious to see what type of play he would adopt, because in the NHL his role was to play aggressively, intimidate opponents, play a defensive style, and on occasion drop the gloves and fight tougher players from the opposing team. In other words, he was an enforcer. Enforcers are often thought to be less skilled because of the role they play, but in reality, anyone who is able to make it into the NHL is an exceptional athlete and among the best players in the world. Within this elite context of professional sport, however, they are not as skilled as the top players and therefore must survive by utilizing other physical assets, whether strong defensive play or fighting and intimidation.

The matchup for this particular game did not fare well for the Lumber Kings, who had a strong team, but on paper did not have the skill or professional talent that the Alberta team did. What they lacked in skill, however, they made up for in toughness, having local tough guys as well as a professional hockey player who was leading the East Coast Hockey League in penalty minutes that season. Prince George teams historically played a tough brand of hockey where they fought and intimidated other teams, which proved quite effective. I was uncertain how they would approach this particular game, playing against the highly respected Gino Odjick who, like them, was known for his toughness, but was clearly not looking to fight in this tournament setting. I expected the Prince George team to go out playing hard and physical, but in a way that paid respect to this hockey icon. In the end they did, but in a manner that I did not anticipate or relate to as a spectator or former player. What occurred destabilized modern Western conventions of sportsmanship and fair play, conveying instead culturally specific meanings that speak to the specificity of First Nations hockey and the cultures from which it is produced.

As the players came out for warm-up, the fans were already jam packed into the arena, buzzing with excitement at the prospect of seeing Gino play. It was clear from the outset he was an exceptional hockey player and he had a dominating presence on the ice. The game began and all eyes were on him. The superior skills of Gino and the other current and former professionals on his team were quickly evident, and they dominated the play. In response, the Lumber Kings tried to throw this team off their game by increasing their physical play, engaging in verbal confrontations and giving occasional 'cheap shots.' Using such tactics was not a surprise, considering it was likely the only way the Lumber Kings stood a chance to win. What was surprising from my perspective was the game within the game, where certain Lumber Kings players would take turns trying to goad Gino into a fight. In fact, I had asked the tournament organizer and Don if they felt Gino would fight in the tournament and both of them responded saying 'it was not worth it' and 'he had nothing to prove' at this point. In fact it would be a no-win situation for an acclaimed tough guy who had fought some of the toughest players in professional hockey to engage in fight in a local hockey tournament. If he won, it would be expected; if he lost, it would tarnish his tough guy image. I expected then that the Lumber Kings players would play him aggressively and at the very least demonstrate that they would not back down from him. Instead the players were doing whatever they could to draw him into a fight, trying everything from verbal engagement to vicious stick work.

As the game progressed, I found the Lumber Kings' behaviour to be disturbing as they repeatedly confronted Gino, calling him out and trying to get him to fight. It was clear that he did not want to engage in a fight and was striving to avoid any confrontation. He was not intimidated; he simply did not want to waste his time fighting in such an event. His trailblazer status earned him the right to participate in the event on his terms and the persistent attacks against him seemed like an affront on him and all that he stood for as a First Nations hockey player. The menacing strategy of the Lumber Kings finally began to pay off and by the third period they had taken a two-goal lead. They were on the verge of a huge upset, yet they did not relent in their efforts to fight Gino, and by the end of the third period it finally happened.

After being shoved, slashed, and confronted along the boards, Gino finally turned around and faced his opponent, who at the time was one of the toughest players in the East Coast Hockey League. The implications of this intergenerational bout between an aspiring NHL hockey tough guy and this retired NHL player were not lost on anyone, and people stood and watched to see who would win. Typically in a hockey fight, both players throw down their gloves, clutch one another with one hand and try landing a punch with the other. The Lumber Kings player did as expected, but Gino only dropped his left glove, and with his bare left hand grabbed the other player's jersey, and with his gloved right hand proceeded to throw a fury of punches to the players face and head area. The fact that the player was able to withstand the barrage of punches speaks to his toughness, but at the same time, the glove reduced the impact of the blows. If Gino had landed those blows with a typical bare-knuckled fist, the other player would have likely gone down in defeat; but as it was the other player continued fighting and was able to finally throw some landing punches of his own. The players continued to throw punches and then wrestled each other to the ice with Gino falling to the bottom. The officials came in to break up the fight, which was essentially over at that point, and both players were directed to skate off the ice towards their dressing rooms. Gino had received a deep gash over his eye, which was bleeding profusely down his face. He looked up to the screaming fans and gave them his classic toothless smile. Meanwhile, his combatant avoided going to his own dressing room exit door and instead went to Gino's door, waiting for him to skate off the ice. As he stepped off the ice, the opponent grabbed his hand and shook it with utmost respect. The player was thanking him, congratulating him, and for the first time giving him what I thought had been absent throughout the game: respect.

My reactions to the game were once again evidence of me 'not getting it'; I was disconnected from the narrative so that when the punch line occurred, I was sitting there wondering what had just happened. I looked to the crowd around me for guidance; some cheered, some booed, others attempted to get closer to Gino for more pictures or the chance of an autograph. After the fight I spoke with both combatants individually, and their comments were intriguing but not necessarily clarifying. It is unlikely that I can fully appreciate the significance of what transpired, but certain meanings did emerge with greater reflection and persistent discussion with the players. First, after speaking with Gino after the fight, I found out that his combatant was once a student of his in a local youth hockey school. The player had looked up to Gino and considered him to be a mentor. Second, Gino had broken his right hand during the game and was barely able to hold his stick let alone throw a punch. It was for this reason he did not take off his glove during the fight. Third, this was not the first time in a First Nations hockey tournament that players attempted to draw him into a fight. They had the opportunity to fight a legendary NHL tough guy who had only been out of the league for a year, and they were taking advantage of it. A few months after the fight in Prince George I conducted an interview with another longtime NHL player who had played on the same tournament team as Gino. The interview focused primarily on his experiences and motivations playing in First Nations tournaments, but at one point we ended up talking about the fight that occurred at the Lumber Kings tournament. His comments were illuminating:

We went to another tournament, and the first game he [Gino] played, I played in the same tournament against the very same team, and they left me alone completely. His first shift, a guy ran him. It was a non-contact tournament. You know, it's like Dave Schultz[8] way back in the seventies. When he got a little older, he wasn't playing as much; everybody was still trying to take liberties, they were going to fight Dave Schultz – make a name for themselves. Well, Natives look at Gino that way. He is, he was a premier tough guy in the NHL for a long time, and that's why he receives it. And it's too bad, because he can, he plays the game well you know.

According to this person, the players were not disrespecting Gino by doing whatever they could to draw him into a fight; instead it was the high regard they held for him that prompted them to want to fight him. It was an honour for these players to have the opportunity to fight him in that their worth as fighters would be measured against it. The outcome – winning or losing the fight – would be of little significance; by simply fighting him they were demonstrating that they were willing to fight one of the toughest First Nation hockey players ever. The aura around this player was humorously captured by Don in an exchange with his teammates at the bar after the game. He explained to them that he managed to get a copy of the score sheet, which he would alter by replacing his teammate's name with his own so that it would appear as though he had fought with Gino Odjick. Don, who was not known as a fighter, would be able to jokingly tell all his friends back home that he fought this NHL heavyweight.

In acknowledging the special significance of engaging in a fight with a revered NHL enforcer, one also needs to appreciate the sacrifice Gino made by complying to fight. There was nothing he needed to prove. And with a broken hand, he was putting himself at the mercy of his opponent, who already had established himself as one of the toughest First Nations pro hockey players at the time. Yet with all this on the line, Gino gave this upstart a shot, allowing him to demonstrate his worth

---

8 Dave Schultz was one of the most revered and feared NHL enforcers. He played for the Philadelphia Flyers during the 'Broadstreet Bullies' era. Under the helm of Hall of Fame coach Fred Shero, the team developed a winning strategy built around fighting and intimidation. Leading the Flyers was Dave Schultz, who received a remarkable 472 penalty minutes in a single season (NHL.com), which remains the highest penalty total for any player in NHL history.

in front of the crowd. It was for this reason the younger player was so adamant about publically thanking his mentor at the conclusion of the fight. Gino *gave* this player the fight; he did not give it to any of the other players who attempted to fight him. In so doing he was making a statement, saying that this player was worthy of being his opponent and thus bestowing honour upon him. Gino's act displayed sacrificial qualities. He willingly put himself in harm's way solely to give this player the opportunity to fight an NHL legend.

After the game I interviewed Gino in the dressing room. At first he downplayed the fight, saying on two different occasions that they were 'just trying to make a show for the fans.' He then started to explain to me how he broke his finger in the first period and showed me his broken hand. We then moved on to something else until he interrupted me, taking me off guard:

ROBIDOUX: Right, in terms of the other hockey you're playing—
GINO: Who won the fight anyways?
ROBIDOUX: What's that?
GINO: [laughs] Who won the fight between me and that kid?
ROBIDOUX: Well you know what, I had it on video and, I tell you, if you didn't have your glove on, I think you would have KO'd him in about three punches. But—
GINO: But I had those gloves, eh?
ROBIDOUX: Yeah, you hit him about three times pretty hard, and then I think he just caught you with one there right at the end, on that side of your head, but—
GINO: Yeah, I think, I cut myself when I fell, when I tried to throw a punch, and fell down face first on the ice.
ROBIDOUX: Oh, okay.
GINO: It hurt.

It was important to him that I knew what had transpired in the fight and that I did not think he had lost. He did not want to look bad in front of his teammates, the opposing players, and the hundreds of fans who had come to watch him play, which makes his act to engage in the fight that much more significant. It was a selfless act, one that he did not have to do, but did anyway to give this younger player 'a shot.' The fight outcome for the younger player was not as important as simply having the opportunity to fight this legendary tough guy. The players all knew this and I suspect many of the fans did as well. Only after listening to the players' responses to the incident did I slowly begin to 'get it' as well. My initial impressions of the event made little sense to the people I spoke with afterwards, exposing the cracks within my own Western imaginary and assumptions about the globalizing potential of sport. Here, very local meanings were manifested in a manner that was unsettling, yet provocative. This was not just a physical confrontation; it was a sign of respect, honour, and generational reciprocity as Gino enabled the younger player to assert his worth in front of local communities and the larger community of First Nations hockey players and fans. The intensity with which it occurred speaks to the physical approach many First Nations players ascribe to the spirit of First Nations sport in general. In this rather lengthy quote, the longstanding NHL player who played with Gino offered what he understood to be the essence of First Nations hockey:

It's tough. Whatever league you play in, this is how we look at hockey. You can win, you can be a good player, but you have to be able to play hard, I mean tough . . . The Native leagues in the West, where we play just against communities, they [the team managers] bring guys in, all Native guys, from east to north. They'll fly them in like guns for hire to play on these teams. They're very, very physical. It's very physical hockey, to a point – it's carried to a point, and that's it. I mean, you won't get the stupidity that you get in a lot of other [leagues] like the NHL or the minors. [The First Nations leagues will] go to a point and they'll fight, but then it's over. I mean there's nothing extra, the guy will show you his fight, [that] he's willing to fight, and then whether you beat him or not, there's none of that trash-talk you find in a lot of other communities. And on the ice, guys go at it pretty hard and they talk, but when it's over, it's over. You know, I had verbalized to the community about that, how they can give so much of themselves, physically and emotionally, in the game, but when the game's over, it's over. They've done what they can, they've worked as hard as they can, and then they're ready to go on to something else after. They're not moping. They're not thinking, we can't believe we lost. They work as hard as they can, and they're willing to have a smile after the game. And I think white culture could learn from that, that it's not life or death. You know, hockey is a place to prove yourself. Sure, physically, and you give all you have emotionally and mentally, but if it's over and you've done that, you can't reproach yourself for anything. And there's something that can definitely be learned from that. And going to most Native tournaments, the biggest thing you'll find is, whether they're contact or non-contact, there'll be contact, and there'll be stick work, but when it's over, it's over.

It was at the Prince George tournament that these meanings were most apparent, which I accredit to its irreverence, its unapologetic approach to being a hockey tournament, and its sincerity. Being at the events, on ice and during social activities, forced me to rethink my observations and challenge my assumptions. I only scratched the surface of all that was available in terms of local meanings and cultural practices, yet the recognition of my own limited access highlights the destabilizing potential of First Nations hockey played within the influence of Western capitalist sporting ideologies. In these high-price tournaments, players are lured to play for the highest bidder, not unlike the earliest manifestations of professional hockey in North America. But their involvement is embroiled in the cultural specificities of each tournament context. This is the draw of these amazing showcases of First Nations hockey talent, and the reason people who have played professionally in North America and Europe are willing to drive twelve hours by car to play two games (as Gino did for this tournament). The experience was grounded in what the players understood to be meaningful to them, evoking a type of cultural awareness that is interestingly articulated by another former NHL player:

> My dad and I were talking about that on the way here, that hockey is replacing lacrosse in the type of spirit that it gives the people. I mean, that's one reason why these tournaments are held; sure, they're fun, but also, Aboriginals are competitive people within themselves. Like my dad was saying, it's not individually so much, it's collectively. And this replaces what lacrosse was way back; hockey has replaced that, and it's a great sport to play, a great team sport. They can go out there as a nation. I mean when we play in [a certain community], that's their community, they're all Cree. They had at least two hundred fans come down for the game, probably more, and they cheered. They were fervent, I mean hard – they cheered, they screamed, they booed us. We were in the Algonquin territory and we were getting absolutely booed. We felt we were visiting somewhere else.

This particular player had competed all over the world, yet the profoundness of these local hockey experiences resonated with him and his family. The ancestral tensions evoked in the matchup he describes reveal the visceral connection between sport and culture. His connection to an indigenous sport heritage tied to the ancient game of lacrosse has been reborn through hockey, which he sees as embodying First Nations spirit and cultural practices. His comments were reminiscent of those shared with me by the Chief of the Esketemc First Nation, who understood sport to embody the spirit of his people. The high-performance setting of these tournaments did not hinder such embodiment, but for this player, enabled it further. The fierce competition was evidence of the passion the people held for the sport and for their Nations who performed it. It is from here that we can move to the local tournament context, which similarly exhibits the passion and competitiveness I have tried to describe. What these tournaments lack in high-priced talent, they make up for in community spirit and passion, providing further means of cultural enunciation and celebration.

Community-Based Tournaments

The distinction I make between the larger, elite tournaments and the community-based events is not intended to suggest that there are essentially two types of tournaments. The distinction is purely based on a particular tournament regulation that stipulates whether or not players are restricted to playing with their own registered communities. Community-based tournaments, unlike the larger, elite tournaments, require that players play for their home community team; as a result, players cannot be bought by the highest bidder, so the talent tends to be more evenly distributed. Beyond this distinction, local tournaments are as diverse as the communities that host them; some are memorial events established in honour of a deceased community member, while others are large-scale community celebrations with extensive player and fan participation and significant prize money. Over the course of my fieldwork I had the opportunity to attend three community-based events, two of them on multiple occasions. For this section I will focus exclusively on one event, the Northern First Nations Hockey Tournament in Sioux Lookout, Ontario, for the simple reason that at this tournament I was provided with tremendous access and a wealth of experiences that require further attention. While the diversity of these kinds of events should not be overlooked, many generalizations can be applied to the community-based tournament format.

The Northern First Nations Hockey Tournament is a weeklong event that takes place during Ontario public schools' March Break, typically around the third week in March. The first time I attended the event was in 2004. I had already spent close to two years studying First Nations hockey tournaments and heard about this event from many of the players who came from northwestern Ontario. The tournament was advertised as the fourth annual event, but a similar version had been running for over ten years under a different organizing committee and name. The current iteration had begun after the organizer of the original event moved the tournament to the larger city of Thunder Bay, and a new committee emerged in Sioux Lookout to take over where he had left off. The event continues to be the largest First Nations hockey tournament in northwestern Ontario, drawing over thirty teams and providing approximately $40,000 in prize money.

One of the primary reasons this tournament continues to be such a success in the region is its location. Sioux Lookout, a former railway town of just over 5,500 residents, has impressively reinvented itself around a new service-based economy, catering to the needs of northern residents. In particular the town has worked closely with northern First Nations groups to provide services to remote residents and enable community organizations and businesses to get established in the town. Such efforts have been instrumental in attracting funding to develop the airport and hospital, which now service the entire region. As the new 'Hub of the North,' Sioux Lookout is one of the only growing economies and populations in this part of Ontario, in large part because of its established First Nations presence.

The hockey tournament has provided an important function, bringing together people from thirty-one First Nations scattered throughout the massive territory of northwestern Ontario. Most of the teams come from fly-in communities, where access by road is limited to a couple of months of the year when winter roads can be constructed over ice and snow. Community members wishing to leave must take planes or drive over the winter road when possible, but such drives can exceed fifteen hours depending on the location. As a result, most people rarely have the chance to leave their communities even when the road is in place. An event such as the Northern First Nations Hockey Tournament enables people from these remote communities to come together and visit with family and friends they would not otherwise see. As mentioned earlier, the nearby Kenora tournament provided a similar function, but because of its relatively elite status, not all teams or players could participate. The Northern First Nations Hockey Tournament is purely recreational, so any team willing to pay the registration fees is encouraged to participate. Teams from the most remote and sparsely populated communities attend, making it a special event.

When I first arrived in 2004 I went to the arena on the Monday morning around 10:00 a.m. At other tournaments I had attended, play did not typically start until later in the day, but I would go to the arena early to observe the space and look for opportunities to meet tournament organizers who were often already there. To my surprise, when I arrived at this arena it was already bustling with activity and a game was underway. I had, in fact, missed two earlier games, as tournament play commenced at 8:00 a.m. This tournament was like no other I had seen, in that games were scheduled every day from 8:00 a.m. until 10:00 p.m. for six straight days. On the seventh day (championship Sunday), games did not start until 1:00 p.m. and concluded with the final championship game at 5:00 p.m. All games were played at the Sioux Lookout Memorial Arena, which has only one ice surface. In order for all thirty-two teams to play the seventy-nine games, the tournament needed to be scheduled over six days and run day and night. While it would be possible to restrict the number of teams for a more condensed schedule, this did not fit within the tournament philosophy. Actually, the organizing committee was contemplating ways to expand the tournament to forty teams.

I have already mentioned that this tournament community provided me with exceptional access to the event, which gave me the opportunity to learn more about tournament operations and the layered involvement of communities, teams, players, and spectators. There were two reasons this access was made possible. First, I went to the tournament knowing that friends of mine from the community of Sandy Lake would be participating. I had met people from Sandy Lake at the Kenora tournament the year before, and from these contacts was eventually invited to visit the community, much like I did the Esketemc First Nation. I went to learn about hockey in this remote, fly-in community in northwestern Ontario, and in return put on a goaltending clinic for local players. My trip to Sandy Lake turned into much more than a field research opportunity. Community members embraced my students and me, providing us with an unforgettable experience. The tournament in Sioux Lookout was an opportunity for me to visit with the friends that I made while in Sandy Lake and to cheer them on during this event. The length of the tournament was also significant in that it was a week long as opposed to a weekend. The extended time with the players afforded longer and more meaningful interactions, while also providing opportunities to meet new networks of players and community members. More so than at the higher-end tournaments, the people appeared interested in my presence as a researcher studying local hockey practices and approached me to talk about their involvement in hockey. The result was a much more intimate tournament experience, which positively impacted my ability to learn about the tournament and local hockey practices.

The second reason for the superior access I enjoyed at this tournament was that the tournament organizer kindly took time out of her hectic schedule to meet with me and share her insights – about the tournament as well as life in the North more generally. Because this was a weeklong event, I had more opportunities to meet with the tournament organizer, and over time got to know her quite well. By the end of the tournament during my first year, I was invited out with the organizing committee to celebrate the conclusion of the event after a gruelling week of work. Through these informal interactions I gained glimpses into the tournament culture that would not have been possible through typical observation and interviewing techniques. I was able to establish a strong rapport with the tournament committee and participants so that by the second year I was allowed to assist the committee with tournament operations. This type of immersion was more than I could have hoped for when I first started my research, and gave me a real appreciation for all that is involved in putting together such an event and the layers of meaning the event holds for participants.

The tournament organizer, Margaret Kenequanash, is truly an exceptional person. She is a well-respected community leader, currently working as Executive Director of a local Tribal Council. She also served as Chief of her community, which is rare for a woman in this region of Canada. She became involved in the tournament after a friend approached her to assist with some of the tournament organization in 2003. She was officially asked if she could organize the tournament the following year. Her devotion to First Nations peoples and issues, as well as her experience and expertise in public administration, made her an ideal person to organize such a large event. The tournament has thrived under her leadership and despite the hard work involved, she has willingly run the tournament ever since.

The organization and running of this event is an extremely onerous process that Margaret explained was a lot to take on in her first year. In addition to all of the logistical concerns such as arena rental, corporate sponsorship, team registration, and accommodations, the micro-details of tournament schedules, format, and rules were a lot to manage. Margaret explained:

> Once we determine [the standings] after the third round of games, we then need to set up the playoffs. And from there we go into the semi-finals and finals. So the two top teams in each pool go into A side. And the third and fourth of each pool – we have eight pools of four teams each – they go into C side. So it was kind of a real learning experience for me. The majority of the work that I did was basically getting sponsorships, getting teams confirmed, getting the tournament rules and regulations out there. And then it wasn't until then that we had to do the format of the program, like for the hockey, and so that means the pools and that's a new experience for me. So it was really interesting.

Prior to my involvement with the tournament committee, I had not appreciated all of the planning and organization required to run such an event. Yet here I was able to experience firsthand much of what was involved, at least during the tournament itself. I was impressed by the stamina of the staff working every day from 7:00 a.m. until well past 1:00 a.m. Their responsibilities included managing security, scheduling and supervising a long list of volunteers, and keeping track of 640 participants. In this tournament the organizers were extremely sensitive to the wide range of skill levels and tried to organize the schedule so that matchups were not grossly lopsided, ensuring both fairness and a positive experience for all teams.

The organizers of this event took a unique approach in that the focus seemed to be on optimizing the overall experience for all involved, including participants, spectators, and the town itself. Even the formal welcome message printed in the 2005 tournament program differed from similar messages at the performance-based tournaments I had attended. In her welcome, Margaret writes:

> We should not only see this tournament as a social event and an economic boon for Sioux Lookout. We need to change our mentality about how we view this tournament. Our younger generation's positive talents and skills must be promoted and one way to do this is through hockey. Hockey not only provides for a healthy lifestyle by active living through sports and exercise, it also offers our young players a chance to play competitive hockey that is entertaining for the fans who are here to cheer for their teams.

This type of messaging does not take away from the competitive spirit, however, which was rewarded through significant prize earnings. The A-side champions win $16,000 and runners-up receive $10,000; B-side champions earn $5,000 and runners-up $4,000; and C-side champions and runners-up take home $3,000 and $2,000, respectively. These considerable sums should not be seen as extravagant, however; much of the prize money barely covers expenses, considering the extraordinary costs teams incur travelling to Sioux Lookout and staying there for a week. Much like other tournaments, the prestige of winning the event carries more weight than monetary rewards.

The combination of competition and positive experience was not simply tournament rhetoric; these combined sensibilities were manifested in tournament play, as I observed on numerous occasions throughout the week. One incident was especially telling. Sometimes at the outset of a game, a recently deceased individual would be honoured by a team from that person's community. The players would be called to line up on their respective blue lines and an announcement would be made. Spectators would stand and mark two minutes of silence in honour of the deceased. On one occasion (there were at least six over the course of the two years I attended), the deceased was a former prominent band councillor and a highly respected member of the community. Typically the game would commence as soon as the two minutes of silence had been observed, but on this occasion the players from the opposing team began offering their individual condolences to the mourning players. They skated up to each one and shook his hand. It was quite moving to watch the players express their sympathies to this team who had only found out that morning that of one of their Elders had passed away. Finally the players returned to their benches and the game commenced. Less than a minute in, the team who had just offered their condolences took the puck, went down the ice and scored. In the end, they mercilessly routed their opponents. They played their hardest, just as they would in any other game, which seemed to indicate a respect for each other, their tournament, and the sport.

It was in this spirit that the tournament was played: fiercely, but with a mutual respect. This was articulated most succinctly on another night, after one team had just lost in a semifinal game on what was a disputed play. I recorded the event in my field notes:

With three minutes left in the third period, A team was winning 4–3. An A-team breakaway then happened but the player was hauled down. The referee signaled for a penalty and the only question was whether he was going to issue a tripping/hooking penalty or a penalty shot. A melee then broke out on the play in front of the net, which caused a distraction. It was quickly broken up and then a faceoff was set up. In breaking up the melee, however, the referee forgot to then issue the penalty he had initially signaled. A team was already on the power play and if a penalty shot was not awarded, they would go on a two-man advantage. But the referee's failure to issue the penalty, which would have carried the rest of the game, gave B team a better chance to make a comeback. Sure enough, the puck was dropped and B team went down the ice and scored the tying goal. They then got the go-ahead goal with a minute left. The game ended with B team winning, and a brief brawl broke out at the conclusion of the game when the players were shaking hands.

I could not believe the turn of events and the fact that the no one from the A team was protesting the play. Either the players had not realized that a penalty was called or they did not consider it worthwhile to challenge; as a result, A team was out of the tournament. Immediately following the game I went to the coaching staff and talked to them, trying to get some sense of their reaction to what had happened. I eventually asked them if they were not upset by the 'blown call.' They had not been aware that a call was initially made, and from our discussion considered protesting the result. While the coaching staff considered what action to take, the assistant coach turned to me and said, 'It was a great game though, eh? We always have this rivalry. We love it. We call them our cousins.' His response blew me away. I like to think of myself as an exponent of fair play and sportsmanship, yet this level of respect was something I had never encountered and could barely comprehend. His comment once again exposed the distinctive meanings available within First Nations hockey, which I tended to universalize as hockey experiences but was clearly failing to grasp. Through conversations such as this, local meanings were made known to me, exposing new ways of thinking about sport and the production of knowledge. I discovered that the mistake made by the official was relatively insignificant in comparison to the overall positive experience and opportunity for the two teams to compete against one another. In fact the term 'compete' poorly captures the magnitude of what these team are actually doing. The act is more fractious, more meaningful than what academics define as a 'process that occurs when rewards are given to people on the basis of how their performances compare with the performances of others doing the same task or participating in the same event' (Coakley 1994, 78). In this tournament hockey is an expression of mutual identification and respect that intensifies with heightened engagement. The act generates meanings for those sharing in the collectivity of hockey, yet from my own Western epistemic, all I could see was a 'blown call' and one team 'unfairly' losing.

There were other distinctive features of this tournament that were remarkable because of their juxtaposition against seemingly main-stream sporting practices. While watching tournament play with friends of mine from Sandy Lake, my friends would occasionally point out important details about the tournament, teams, players, and playing styles. At one point, a friend mentioned that the game we were watching was between two small communities with popula-tions of less than five hundred people each. He explained that these smaller communities only had outdoor rinks and did not have access to organized hockey. What struck me as odd, then, was that many of the players had high-end hockey equipment: skates upwards of $700; graphite hockey sticks close to $200; and custom-designed hockey jerseys, which typically run about $75 each or roughly $1,200 for the team. If they only played loosely organized recreational games on outdoor rinks, this high-end equipment seemed impractical. In stark contrast to these flashy new jerseys and equipment, many of the other players had lower-end and even makeshift gear; there was a wide range in the quality of equipment in use, even among players on the same team. As we watched the players warm up, they began performing a variety of drills typically seen in professional hockey games. Players immediately went to the side boards and did the ubiquitous groin stretch. This was followed by passing and shoot-ing drills and then a high-tempo skate to conclude. The players were clearly attempting to embody the professional hockey aura, yet any appearance of professionalism was erased through failed execution. For example, when players would go in and shoot on the goalie, their shots were often high and wild. This erratic shooting is not so much a comment on skill, but breaks one of the most basic tenets in hockey: never risk injuring your goaltender. Not only did players shoot high at their goaltender, they would shoot when he was not looking or when his back was turned. On more than one occasion, I saw a goal-tender get hit in the back or back of the leg, the only unprotected area on his body. Players would not go over and apologize, signifying the somewhat regularity of such an occurrence. Elite goaltenders will often react to such carelessness by skating over to their teammates and slashing them hard with their stick to let them know they had better not do that again.

Another example of the incongruence between the professionally emulated warm-up and its amateur execution could be seen with one small community team that was performing similar warm-up drills when their two coaches came on the ice and began doing the drills with the players. The coaches were dressed in their street attire, all in black to match their team's jerseys, but they wore skates. On the ice they led their players through the remainder of the drills. When the warm-up was over, they went behind the bench and coached the entire game with their skates still on. The distinctiveness of these local styles carried over into the game itself where even the Sandy Lake players I sat with would remark that a player must be living 'in town' because of his superior skills and knowledge of the game. In other words, one could tell who had access to organized hockey, which contrasted with the pond-style hockey most participants played. Players were emulating dominant Western sporting practices, but rather than simply reproducing the global, they were enunciating the local in the global through their own unique interpretations. What must be understood here is that local performances were not perceived as flawed representations of the dominant Western style of play. Instead, these local formulations of global designs were privileged as more expressive and meaningful styles of play. On numerous occasions while watching the games and engaging in hockey chatter, my friends and I would comment on nice plays, good saves, and what I saw as 'missed opportunities.' I would see a player skating with the puck choose not to move it to an open player in an advantageous position; instead, he would carry the puck and stickhandle through one or more opponents. Such individual plays run counter to modern coaching strategies, which maximize efficiency and minimize risk. A pass is more effective because the puck can move faster than the player, and risk is minimized by feeding the puck to a second offensive player, preventing a one-on-one encounter. On one occasion while watching a game with a friend from Sandy Lake, we had the following exchange:

ROBIDOUX: They're not finding the open guy.
SL: Not passing?
ROBIDOUX: Yeah.
SL: Isn't that boring? Up and down all the time.

He was right. System-based styles of play are boring compared to the creative risk-taking versions of the game where players face off one on one, leading in most cases to turnovers and eventual scoring opportunities. The player I was speaking with had lived in Ottawa briefly and played on a Junior B hockey team, so he had, to a certain extent, experienced playing in the highly regimented North American style of the game. My comment was coming from the same Western sport model that had little relevance in this type of tournament. The accoutrements of professional hockey were present in the stylized jerseys, high-end equipment, and mimetic performances of warm-up drills, yet were similarly distorted through localized expressions of sport. A final carryover was seen in the stands, where a young child wore a miniature version of his community team's customized jersey. The popular Western phenomenon of supporting one's favourite team by purchasing and donning the team jersey is wonderfully expressed here; but this child boasts not an Ottawa Senators or a Montreal Canadiens jersey, but a Deer Lake jersey with a logo appropriated from the Calgary Hitmen of the Canadian Western Hockey League. The borders of global practices are wonderfully exposed and manipulated through gestures such as this, giving way to powerful expressions of cultural identity.

The manifestations of local practices in the face of large global structures were most evident in the community-based events such as the Northern First Nations Hockey Tournament. The teams were community based, and the players were performing for – and as – their communities. Through their actions players represented their communities, and whatever successes they achieved would extend to the community as a whole. The stands were filled with community members cheering for their teams, and if their own community was knocked out they would stand and cheer for teams with which they held some affiliation. Even teams that were already eliminated but were simply playing out the remainder of their games had fans cheering them on and proudly displaying signs and banners of support. During a C-side game, one team had only six players; just enough to put out one line and a goaltender. Without any substitutes it was impossible for them to compete with the other team, but they went out and played as hard as they could despite their inevitable fate. At one point a scrum occurred in front of their net and one of their players was ejected from the game. With only four skaters, they had to play out the rest of the game a player short. Rather than weakening their resolve, however, this inspired them to compete even harder. As the game concluded I recorded the following:

The team without enough players ended up losing 6–3. At one point they had to kill a penalty playing two men short yet still they made a game of it. At the end the players met in a huddle with the goalie in the crease and bowed on their knees, almost in prayer or giving thanks. They threw up their hands in victory, as if their shorthanded effort was a feat deserving of applause and recognition. It was, actually, and the fans cheered. Their effort was honourable and they knew this. The fans responded with cheers. The long-haired, flamboyant goalie stayed on the ice, throwing his arms up as if to say 'we have honour! We played hard despite the odds! Recognize this!' It was an amazing display.

Although the Sioux Lookout arena could fit no more than eight hundred to a thousand fans, the level of intensity at this event was unparalleled, even when compared with the larger tournaments I attended. As the tournament progressed, so too did fan intensity and enthusiasm. In the evenings the arena would get jam packed with people working their way along the rafters to get a view of the game. When a goal was scored the stands would erupt with deafening cheers. It was truly a collective experience as men and women of all ages joined in celebrating their own and each other's communities through hockey. Standing amongst the fans, barely able to move and engulfed in passionate cheers, I felt I was part of something special. The importance of this event could not have been more evident as I watched people engage passionately in the tournament experience and the hockey that was being performed in front of them.

Conclusion

In this chapter I have described two distinctive First Nations hockey tournament formats: prestigious national events where players from across the country participate and community-based tournaments where teams are formed with players from specific communities. While this division is important, it should not be confused with the overall diversity of the events, whether open or community based. Each tournament I attended had its own special character, providing unique experiences for all levels of participants. I have tried to emphasize the ways in which tournaments align or diverge from dominant Western sporting practices and where local meanings emerge within the modern construct of hockey. As First Nations peoples take up the sport in these diverse settings, specific cultural meanings are expressed. The high-priced elite tournaments, where players receive considerable

sums of money to participate, are valued performances of First Nations excellence and success despite their mercenary framework. The
new informal economy of these tournaments is resisted and exploited,
providing further evidence of the importance of hockey to First Nations peoples as they continually inscribe the sport with new meanings
and values. For some, monetary incentives pose a threat to what are
perceived as locally specific versions of hockey, while others perceive
buying players as testament to these players' exceptional level of skill.
Community-based tournaments maintain local interests as their prior-
ity, offering a distinctive community brand of hockey. The emphasis
on the local provides important opportunities for First Nations people
to come together in inter-community festivities, celebrating their roots
and experiencing the pride associated with playing before their communities. Regardless of the tournament format, First Nations peoples
of all ages embrace the hockey, whether for the skilful performances or
the proud community displays. These tournaments are remarkable in
many ways, yet darker associations, which reflect poorly on First Nations hockey and the cultures and people who play it, persist.

In the next chapter I will focus on some of the darker realities that
exist at these events, in part to avoid romantic delusions that hockey
tournaments are ever free of problematic behaviours, but to also con-
textualize these issues as part of First Nations/Euro-Canadian relations.
First Nations hockey tournaments are embedded in politics of race that
are heightened in many of the small towns where the tournaments take
place. Despite the significant economic benefits these tournaments provide, there are tensions in host towns that play out in a variety of ways.
I will speak to the tensions that I encountered in the hope of offering
insight into problematic behaviours and how they are situated within
the larger colonial imaginary.

4 Constructing the Other through Hockey

On my flight home from one of the tournaments, I was seated next to a pilot who was deadheading back home after completing his shift. He asked about my trip and I told him that I was a professor studying First Nations hockey. He was fascinated with the project and told me that he had grown up living close to four different reserve communities and had played hockey with and against First Nations players and teams. He described First Nations hockey as 'crazy,' and said that as a 'white-guy' he was routinely victimized. He began telling me stories of dangerous encounters where players would attack him and First Nations officials would permit such abuses to occur. He recounted once being 'clobbered' by a First Nations player. While he lay on the ice in pain, the player proceeded to 'tomahawk' him with his hockey stick. The only thing that saved him, he said, was raising his forearm to fend off the blow. The pilot summarized First Nations hockey as 'really different; it's hard to explain, but they play different.'

I was not unfamiliar with this kind of response to my research. Numerous people have responded in similar ways; one such instance occurred shortly after conducting research in the Southern Alberta community of Kainai (see Robidoux 2004).

A former student of mine came to my office to chat and asked what I was working on. I told him research on hockey in Kainai. He responded, 'Oh, that's the place to do it. We always had experiences playing there. Do they still have that old beat up arena?' (They actually have quite a nice facility there.) I asked him if he played minor hockey there. He responded, 'Oh yeah, a few trips there.' He said one time his team only had about eight or nine players and they were really scared. 'You're always scared playing there. They were always more violent. They were always playing some kind of trick on you.' During the one game, he told me, 'one of the players got spit on.' I think he then reflected on how I might be responding to his story and added, 'Not that I have anything against them.' But then he continued: 'They always bring a crowd with them on the road. One time two women got into a fight in Vauxhall. A girl in my sociology class was right in the middle of it.'

First Nations hockey is often portrayed as violent, reckless, and dangerous. During my research in Kainai, I learned how neighbouring non-First Nations minor hockey associations perceived the Kainai team. Claims of cheating and verbal and physical abuse in the stands and on the ice filled pages of complaints from parents that one hockey association filed against the Kainai association. The persistent complaints and the severity of the alleged offences eventually led to Kainai's banishment from minor hockey, which was only remedied when Kainai joined a different league the following year.

Stereotypical characterizations of First Nations people are not new; early European accounts were mixed with fear and contempt for what they perceived as a barbaric lifestyle. Descriptions of First Nations recreation are especially telling; early missionaries, colonialists, and settlers openly described their disdain for what they saw as an excessively violent and overzealous approach to sport. One of the earliest accounts comes from Nicolas Perrot (1973) who encountered the game of lacrosse while living as a *coureur de bois*[1] between 1665 and 1684 in eastern Canada. He writes:

One can hear the noise they make when they hit one another, while they attempt to avoid receiving blows in order to throw the ball to a favourable location. If one secures the ball in his feet without letting it go, he must fend off blows from his opponents who continually strike his feet; and if in this situation he is injured, it is his own concern. Some are seen with broken legs or arms, or are even killed as a result. It is common to see players maimed permanently, yet this does not change the way they play the game on account of their obstinacy.[2] (45; my translation)

---

1 Literally means 'runner of the woods.' More specifically, *coureurs des bois* were French male fur traders and trappers who lived as the indigenous population did during the seventeenth century. Miller writes that these young males were 'neither French peasants nor Indian braves, they were a bit of both' (2000, 56).
2 'Vous entendez le bruit qu'ils font en se frapant les uns contre les autres, dans le temps qu'ils veulent parer les coups pour envoyer cette boule du costé favorable.

Constructions of First Nations peoples as barbaric and wild have persisted throughout North American history. Beginning in the 1870s, representations of First Nations savagery proliferated in the wild west genre, as seen in literature (Bugmann 2008), live theatre (Kasson 2000; Moses 1996), and later film (Deloria 2004). While popular culture offered powerful imagery that produced and maintained negative stereotypes of First Nations culture, other media also contributed to derogatory Euro-North American understandings of First Nations peoples. For example, early marketing campaigns designed to sell vacations to the Canadian Rocky Mountains relied on imagery that temporalized local First Nations as 'wild,' 'natural,' and 'savage' (Mason 2008). Along with meeting tourists' expectations, these discourses positioned First Nations on the margins of Canadian society and were later used to deny local communities access to considerable resources (Mason 2009, 2010).

These negative portrayals of First Nations peoples persist in contemporary popular cultural forms, most notably the endless parade of mascot and team logo imagery in professional and collegiate sport. These images, such as the Cleveland Indians' Chief Wahoo logo, are based on First Nations stereotypes and caricatures (Davis 1993; Franks 1982; Guggenheim 1998; King and Springwood 2001; Pewewardy 1991; Sigelman 1998; Slowikowski 1993; Staurowsky 1998). The menacing images displayed on team jerseys and performed through mascots perpetuate wild and violent stereotypes of First Nations people. Whether it is a Native warrior with spear tearing up and down the football field at a Florida State game or the visual and linguistic offence generated by the Washington Redskins, the disparaging construct of indigenousness is profound. In this chapter I will examine how these constructs of First Nations people permeate First Nations tournament hockey, and critically examine some of the more destructive behaviours I encountered over the course of the fieldwork. The purpose is not to reinforce the stereotype of First Nations tournaments as excessively violent or riddled with social problems, but rather to expose the issues and challenges tournament organizers and communities face in running these events.

Quand quelqu'un la garde entre les pieds sans la vouloir lascher, c'est à luy d'eviter les coups que ses adversaires luy portent sans discontinuer sur les pieds; et s'il arrive dans cette conjoncture qu'il soit blessé, c'est pour son compte. Il s'en est veü, qui ont eü les jambes cassées, d'autres les bras, et quelques uns ont estez mesme tüez. Il est fort ordinaire d'en voir d'estropiez pour le reste de leurs jours, et qui ne l'ont esté qu'à ces sortes de jeu par un effect de leur opiniâtreté' (Perrot 1973, 45).

Encountering Perceptions of First Nations Hockey Tournaments

Up until this point I have emphasized the positive attributes of First Nations hockey tournaments, but the local populations in the hosting towns do not always share these views. In fact, the tournaments often face criticism from local residents and authorities who claim these events propagate violence, excessive drinking, and public calamity. One account dating back to 1972 highlights the economic incentive for hosting a tournament, but the potential benefits are overshadowed by allegations of unruly behaviour. The passage comes from the *Saskatchewan Indian* (1972) and captures the tensions that can exist during tournament events:

> One of the best Indian Hockey tournaments take [*sic*] place in North Battleford . . . North Battleford is surrounded by reserves and a great deal of trade takes place between the two communities not to mention the amount of business brought by the hockey tournament alone . . . The final indignity came Saturday night. The R.C.M.P. parked a bus on the street outside the Auditorium Hotel. About eight cops then proceeded to pick up every Indian who might have had too much to drink even though these people had rooms in the very hotels they were drinking in . . . When the reign of terror was finished, over 100 Indian people had been arrested and dragged off to jail. Waiters were seen escorting their customers to the door where the police took them to the bus. If Indian activities are fair game for the police what about other activities such as the exhibition at Regina and Saskatoon? What about the Grey Cup game; which is little more than a sanctioned drunk?

The passage is noteworthy in that it points to the financial gains for local businesses during First Nations hockey tournaments. Few formal assessments have measured the economic impact of adult tournaments, but a major youth tournament held recently in Sudbury reportedly brought in millions to local hotel, restaurant, and retail businesses. In promoting the return of this First Nations youth hockey tournament, the City of Sudbury made the following statement: '118 teams from across Ontario are expected to attend the four-day tournament, attracting close to 5,000 players and spectators and an estimated economic spin-off of $5 million . . . Shelly says it's anticipated the Little NHL Hockey Tournament will require 7,500 hotel room nights in the Greater Sudbury area. Restaurants, service providers and entertainment facilities are also anticipating a steep rise in business this March' (Sudbury 2002). For remote towns and cities looking for economic development, the tournaments are an attractive option. Yet despite these economic spinoffs, the tournaments are overshadowed by allegations of intense social activities involving excessive alcohol consumption and occasional violence.

In response to these allegations, it is worth examining how this behaviour is different from what takes place at any other major sporting event in North America, where alcohol consumption and tailgate parties are marketed as part of the overall experience. I spent three years conducting field research at these tournaments, and the behaviour I observed was no more extreme than anything I encountered growing up playing amateur and recreational hockey in Ontario. Yet First Nations tournament organizers and participants must contend with these negative stereotypes, which shape the way they market their events. Most events are now alcohol free, meaning alcohol is not served onsite and anyone showing signs of intoxication is immediately removed. In addition, the tournaments are advertised as community gatherings or festivals rather than hockey tournaments in an attempt to prevent the negative associations with violence and substance abuse. A vivid example of this is seen in a description of the Sioux Lookout tournament before it became the Northern First Nations Hockey Tournament. In the 1990s the tournament organizers deliberately shifted the tournament's image from that of a standard hockey tournament to a family-friendly social event:

> Then came March, the month of the Northern Bands hockey spectacular. After seeing the alcohol abuse associated with the 'big' hockey tournament in previous years, the committee wanted to offer an alternative form of social gathering during this year's tournament. It would be a social gathering where people could come and go as they pleased, where the whole family could be involved . . . The time can be had without the use of alcohol or any other drug, and where a fee wasn't required to enter. And certainly it would be a gathering where one could gain a sense of pride in being Anishnawbe. (Henry 1996)

These efforts, however, have not fully erased the negative stereotypes participants and organizers face, which I observed while attending the tournaments.

My very first tournament, in Brandon, Manitoba, exposed me to one element of the discrimination and put my students and me in an uncomfortable situation. After trying to get rooms in every hotel and motel in the city, I started calling bed and breakfasts. They too were full, but the owner of the third one began explaining to me why everything was at capacity. He said it was on account of the 'Native' tournament that would be going on that weekend. I explained to him that it was not by coincidence I was travelling to Brandon, as I was a university professor conducting a study on the tournament. Surprisingly the bed and breakfast owner responded by saying that his establishment was no longer full and that he would be able to accommodate us after all. He even offered to pick us up at the airport in Winnipeg, a four-hour return trip from Brandon. I was slightly uncomfortable with this sudden turnaround, intuiting that we were only being accepted as guests because we were not First Nation hockey players. Without any other options, however, I simply thanked him for taking us in. On the second day of our stay, the owner brought up our telephone conversation, as if apologizing for his seemingly discriminatory guest policy. He informed us that he had nothing against Native people, but did not want to have loud partying hockey players in his house. A few hours later he spoke about the abject poverty many First Nations communities are facing, and said that the Canadian government could not be expected to keep doling out money to take care of them. A year later, I faced a similar reaction when seeking accommodations at a bed and breakfast in Sioux Lookout, Ontario. Only after I confirmed that I was not a First Nations hockey player was I able to book a room at his establishment.

The negative perceptions of tournament hockey are not entirely baseless, as there are issues of excessive alcohol consumption, violence, and other social problems. These behaviours are present in varying degrees at each tournament, not unlike what one would find at any sport-centred celebratory event. The behaviours are not emblematic of the tournaments, however, and should not override the multitude of experiences that are far more predominant. For example, every event is an important site for intergenerational and intercommunity gatherings, fostering strong social ties and pride in local cultural practices. The ability of tournaments to bring people together is often cited as the reason people keep coming back. On numerous occasions Elders I met at the tournaments would tell me how important these events were for visiting friends and family from other communities who they would otherwise not see. For others it was a chance to be part of the First Nations hockey experience. One man from a remote reserve community in northern Saskatchewan was a huge fan of the Prince George Lumber

Kings and went to tremendous lengths to attend the tournament and see them play. He had limited economic resources, so Harley and his team members would often help him out, either by assisting him with lodging or covering some of his meals. This man's devotion to the Lumber Kings earned him a spot as team 'trainer,' allowing him to spend as much time with the players as possible. During my first year at the tournament, he was presented with a plaque at the post-championship game celebration demarcating the team's victory, a gesture that clearly moved him. He then went around the room with a Vancouver Canucks NHL jersey asking all of the Prince George Lumber Kings players to sign it. These are just some of the many examples of the special significance the tournaments hold. But it is important for two reasons to also acknowledge problematic behaviours that are present. First, it rejects any pretence that the tournaments are somehow disconnected from other social realities, both good and bad. Second, making sense of the darker side of these events will help to dispel any notions that negative aspects of the tournaments are somehow particular to First Nations events or culture. The fact that these behaviours exist is not so much the issue; it is the fact that when they occur they feed into disparaging stereotypes and racist ideologies of First Nations peoples.

Violence

Prior to commencing the fieldwork for this study, I had met people who played hockey with or against First Nations players and who tended to characterize First Nations hockey as inherently aggressive and violent. During the tournaments themselves some of the spectators would speak of the violence that they had witnessed at previous tournaments, and indicated that they were expecting to see fights and violent bodychecks at this one as well. What transpired over the course of my fieldwork, however, was very different from what I had heard about the tournaments and what some of the onlookers were expecting. In the previous chapter I alluded to incidents of violence and fighting that extended into the stands, but these were isolated incidents. I attended over five hundred tournament hockey games over three years of fieldwork, and with a few exceptions, the events were remarkably devoid of fighting or excessively violent and aggressive play. Contrary to the stereotype of First Nations hockey as wild and unruly, the players showed a restraint one does not typically see in dominant North American versions of the sport. If anything, the behaviour on the ice was more sportsmanlike

than what I was accustomed to from my experience playing and watching Euro-Canadian hockey. Or rather, the behaviour was sportsmanlike
in appearance, as what was taking place had little to do with Western
constructs of fair play, gentlemanly behaviour, and sportsmanship.

Stating that game play was relatively devoid of violence is not to
suggest that the play was lacking in physical intensity or competive-
ness. Players used physical domination and intimidation tactics, but
these behaviours rarely escalated into anything beyond a brief shoving match. I began documenting occurrences of fierce engagement between players, which I initially described as pretexts to fights. At times
players would give others a jab with their stick or slash them, but their
opponents would rarely retaliate. During one particularly rough but
uneventful (at least in terms of fighting or excessive violence) game,
I wrote in my field notes:

*There is a lot of physical posturing but very little escalation into fighting.
There seems to be a value associated with physical bravado and intimidation,
but it has a different meaning here. If I were playing and a guy gave me a cheap
shot or pushed me, I would think it was a direct invitation to something more,
possibly a fight. Here the pushing and challenging does not seem to be interpreted so literally by the other player. It is recognized as posturing but rarely
elicits a truly confrontational response.*

It was clear from watching the play and speaking with players that
toughness and physical prowess were highly valued qualities. In an
interview with Don, he stated:

I'm sure you remember player x and player z; they played for the United
League. In 1995 their cousin was playing defence for a different team and
player z knocked him out cold, for five minutes at least, at centre ice with
a clean hit. He just picked up the puck, he was going up to beat the man,
and he had his head down, and his own cousin – like they were first cousins and he fuckin' drilled him – he killed him. He went right over, boom!
Rammed right over him, and he knocked him out. He didn't move for like
five minutes, and they had the ambulance and everything come out . . .
But this particular hit, the guy cried, and man I'll never forget it because
it happened right in front of our bench. He was drilled straight on, and he
knocked him out, and that's his own cousin.

The point of Don's narrative was to illustrate how physical play is dep-
ersonalized, a feature of the sport, not something one should lose one's

temper over, or for which to seek atonement – which is standard in North American professional hockey. When a player receives a punishing blow in professional hockey – legal or not – his teammates typically respond by confronting the player who delivered the hit and challenging him to a fight, or at the very least offering threats of retribution. Reflecting on what I was seeing at the Brandon tournament, I wrote:

> *If anything, the roughness seems to be expected and mutually understood. I don't think there was one incident of someone losing their temper in all the games. There were some nasty hits, and some quite dangerous, but not once was there a strong negative reaction. That's quite remarkable and I would say runs counter to Euro-Canadian hockey where similar incidents would create some kind of confrontation.*

With the hit Don was describing, he said the players were expressing concern about their fellow player's well-being, 'because obviously nobody wants to see anyone get hurt. So once that initial reaction happens, then everybody's helping him out, making sure he gets carried off or whatever, and hoping he's all right.'

Over the course of my fieldwork, I documented a total of two brawls and one game where multiple fights took place simultaneously. The incidents were quite intense and in one case the police were called. Considering how many games I observed, however, this type of fighting proved to be extremely rare. What is noteworthy is that these were not typical hockey fights; the violence was generated by the larger context surrounding the games. In the brawl that occurred in Kenora, the fans from one community felt that the older players from the other team were bullying their players, which triggered verbal and later physical interventions from the stands. In the theatre of North American professional sport, the fans do not have the influence to directly affect on-ice behaviour. Violence may break out in the crowd, but it is relatively independent of on ice play. The fans in Kenora, however, were community members – they were an extension of the team and therefore had the ability to directly affect what occurred on the ice. Spectators challenged the other team and their fans, which eventually led to the brawl. The brawl that occurred in Prince George also had more to do with the context than the game itself. The match involved two communities who had throughout history been embroiled in conflict, and the fight was a reflection of these ongoing tensions. The previous year, these two teams had been unable to finish their game because of the fighting that broke out between players and fans. The year I attended there was a line brawl and fans verbally interacted with players who were engaged in the fighting. Within ten minutes the entire incident was over; some players were ejected from the game, order was restored, and the game resumed. Other isolated incidents of violence I observed during tournament play were similarly innocuous; no major injuries were sustained and teams were able to continue their involvement in the tournament without incident.

Players who had participated in these tournaments for years explained to me that what I was seeing was not an aberration, and more than anything, tournament play was a gathering amongst family and friends, an escape from larger social realities. As Don explained,

> There's not only pride for us, it's pride for your aunt, uncle, or cousin who you are watching. Because it's kind of a common thread . . . you know, the common thread is hockey. When the tournament's over, bang, you know, everybody goes to the lounge and talks about the breakaway that someone scored or missed, or made a save . . . Like it's just a common thing where you kind of put the barriers, political – whatever you call it – aside, and people can agree to put that other shit away for the time being. It will continue in a couple days, but for now, let's just enjoy the camaraderie and competitiveness of hockey.

My three years of tournament observations dispelled any conceptions of First Nations hockey as excessively violent or dangerous. Any isolated incidents of violence that did occur on the ice ended with the game. Off the ice, however, there were incidents of violence that proved to be more distressing than anything at the rinks. These incidents took place at social events, dances, bars, or nightclubs, and under the influence of alcohol.

Before speaking to these incidents, I want to offer my own personal narrative about playing in a (non-Aboriginal) recreational hockey tournament in Ottawa, Ontario, in the summer of 2006. The tournament was a fundraising event and involved adult recreational teams who placed first or second in their winter recreational leagues. Our team was made up of some university professors as well as some of our current and former students and their friends. We were playing in the highest division of the tournament, but it was purely recreational – no bodychecking and no monetary prizes. The event started on a Friday evening and we won our first game. We won our second game on Saturday morning and advanced to a playoff game scheduled for 5:00 that evening. After the morning game, our team went upstairs to the bar and ordered pitchers of beer. I left after a couple of glasses to get a few things done at home. When I returned to the rink for our evening game, there were only four members of our team in the dressing room. We wondered where our missing teammates were – they were also our best players. Ten minutes before the game was to begin, four of our players entered the dressing room shirtless, sunburnt, and completely inebriated. After leaving the arena bar, these younger players had found their way to a friend's party and spent the day drinking poolside. Any hope of actually winning the game was completely lost, but for most of us that was of little concern – we were happy just to be playing.

When our team skated onto the ice for warm-up, we knew we were in trouble. A couple of our players were having a hard time even skating, let alone playing the game. Within minutes our opponents scored on us and one of the more intoxicated players skated through centre ice, fell to his knees, and slid across the ice, waving his sticking as though kayaking across the red line. The referee gave the player a warning to cease with the antics, but to no avail. Midway through the first period this player was ejected from the game for directing a nonsensical verbal assault at the referee, who had already put up with too much folly from him. The game only degenerated from there. By the third period we were down by four or five goals, and one of the intoxicated players got into a shoving match with an opposing player. As they were shoving, the intoxicated player's brother (also intoxicated) approached the opposing player and, using his stick as a pitchfork, stuck the player, lifted him completely off the ice, and slammed him down. With this, the opposing player's teammates came in to intervene, at which point they were approached by the remaining intoxicated player. In a flash, one of the players was grabbed, his helmet was thrown off, and he was punched to the head, his nose splitting open. He dropped to the ice with blood pouring from his face. While all of this was going, I was watching from our bench. It was not the first time I had seen something like this, and likely will not be the last. The intoxicated players were eventually ejected from the game thus ending the chaos, and once all the penalties were assessed the match resumed.

I offer this narrative to illustrate the strong connection that exists between recreational hockey and alcohol, and the pervasiveness of violent, unruly behaviour in hockey – these aspects of the game are not specific to or more prevalent in First Nations contexts. The reference to recreational hockey leagues as beer leagues is no misnomer; games are in most cases followed by alcohol consumption, whether in the dressing rooms or at a local sports bar. Tournaments are even more notorious for alcohol consumption, as teams spend the weekend together playing multiple games followed by multiple drinking sessions that tie into other weekend festivities. First Nations tournaments are no different, even if they are dry events prohibiting the sale or consumption of alcohol on arena grounds. Many players look at tournament weekends as mini-vacations away from their home communities, where they can partake in the celebratory and social activities associated with the event. For some players and fans who come from communities where alcohol is prohibited, the tournaments are rare opportunities to legally purchase and consume alcohol and visit bars and nightclubs. They are also some of the few times of the year when this type of social behaviour is possible for people from remote communities. Most tournaments hold dances, which players described as a vital component of the tournament experience. A long-time NHL player now playing in the tournaments explained,

> It centres around the tournament itself, but also around the dance that goes on . . . where everybody talks about the women dancing, talking, having a few drinks, whatever it may be . . . That's an important part; every tournament has a social evening, and if they don't, it's kind of odd. They try to organize something.

Teams that are able to moderate their drinking fare better in the tournament. My teammates in the Ottawa tournament did not restrain themselves, but with nothing on the line it was of little consequence to our team. For players like Don, however, managing the social component of the tournament is critical. He explained in one interview:

> You know like, Ivan, I might see him a couple times a year. We've known each other for ten years and we've won quite a few hockey tournaments together – probably about twenty for sure. Just like Brandon this year, you try and maintain the not drinking, only because you want to win. Not because you don't want to go out . . . hey, why else would you want to go [to the tournament]? To get away from the old lady, go hit the bar and reminisce and have the beer that you couldn't have when you were playing for real [when playing junior hockey]. It is hard not to, you know, like the guy in the red helmet, he says, 'Come on, let's go out.' I said, 'Ok, well I'm not

gonna drink, but I'll go out.' So I went to the bar and I was ordering vodka sevens because it looked like water, because I didn't want all the other players seeing me double fisting beer, you know, because they'd be like, 'Hey listen, you just gave us a speech about not drinking, look at him.' And then, you know, they take it overboard. Because, you know, boozing is going to happen, it's no different [than non-First Nation hockey]. I'm gonna go out that's just the way it is.

Throughout my fieldwork, participating in the tournaments' social activities often led to my most meaningful dialogue with players, spectators, and organizers. These occasions were also some of the most memorable and enjoyable experiences I had at the tournaments. Much of the socialization took place in sports bars, night clubs, and after-hours parties and involved high levels of alcohol consumption. It was during these excessive drinking events that destructive behaviours surfaced.

These destructive behaviours took many forms, most often alcohol/ substance abuse or violent late-night fights. Accounts of fights that took place during tournament weekends were often featured in the post-game storytelling sessions. Interestingly, however, these stories were rarely recounted merely to rehash the details of the fights; they generally included some defining element that prompted the narrative, as in the case of Don's story about Harry, who, while pummelling someone on the ground, yelled, 'Who's Hairy now?' Other stories focused on fights that led to extremely violent outcomes, violence against women, or incidents of racism – or a combination of all three. I came across various examples of these more extraordinary and tragic events either through narrative or firsthand.

I heard about one extreme incident the morning after the tournament dance in Prince George, while watching a game on championship Sunday. Two women who appeared to be in their early twenties sat down in front of me, beside an older man. I could hear their conversation clearly. One of the women began telling the man, who was her grandfather, about the previous night. She started by saying that she had just come from the hospital where she had multiple staples put in her head to close a large gash. She received the gash trying to protect her friend (the woman beside her) from her ex-boyfriend, who was beating her up at the bar. She told her grandfather that the ex-boyfriend punched her friend in the face numerous times, giving her black eyes and a broken nose. She showed her grandfather her friend's battered face. She continued that when she had intervened in the fight, her friend's ex-boyfriend had taken a beer bottle and smashed it over her head. She showed her grandfather the staples in her head. At this point another female friend approached and they continued discussing the incident. It was revealed that the ex-boyfriend was a police officer who worked on one of the local reserves. The grandfather offered little reaction to the story, nor did the woman who had just arrived. This woman changed the subject to recount her story from the previous night. She had been working as a waitress at one of the main nightclubs. Once the dance was over, people showed up at the bar and fights broke out, which eventually carried out into the streets. The fights went on until 4:30 in the morning. She concluded by saying, 'but they weren't as bad as last year.'

The following year in Sioux Lookout I encountered another incident while at a local bar with friends. A player from another team came over and started talking to some of the guys at our table. They introduced me to him and explained that I was doing a study on First Nations hockey, to which the man took my hand, warmly shook it, and told me a couple of tournament stories. When he left I started laughing and explained that the previous night, my student and I had been at this bar playing pool. During our game, the guy who I had just been introduced to approached our pool table, extremely intoxicated. He proceeded to take the balls from our table and crash them into other balls to disrupt our game. Meanwhile he was looking at me, and he began challenging me to a fight. As I stood there wondering what to do, the waitress came over and scolded the guy, telling him to leave us alone or she would throw him out of the bar. As I told the story I emphasized the fact that the waitress was half my size and weight and had amazingly come to my rescue. (In truth her intervention was greatly appreciated, as I had not been certain how the event would play out.) The guys laughed and teased me about being saved by the waitress, but quickly pointed out that this guy was a 'gentle giant' and would not hurt a fly, which was likely why the waitress handled the situation so easily. At the same time my friends appeared to be sensitive to the fact that I, as a Caucasian from southern Ontario, had been confronted in such a way. In response to my story, the guys started describing a darker reality of interracial violence that they had experienced in northern Ontario towns.

One incident had occurred earlier that week, when one of the players was hurt badly by two non-First Nations men at the same bar. It was late at night and the First Nations man was extremely intoxicated. The two Caucasian men approached him and began making fun of him and how inebriated he was. Eventually he was pushed to the ground and the two men began kicking him to the head and face with their boots. There was no one in the bar capable of intervening, and when they had had their fill the two men simply left the guy lying in a pool of blood on the floor. My friends explained that it was typical at events like this for white men to come out late at night looking to take advantage of vulnerable First Nations people and commit acts of violence. I cannot verify the veracity of this particular incident as it was only recounted secondhand. I report it because I experienced a similar incident two years later at the same local tavern in Sioux Lookout after meetings on a different research project. After the meetings, a colleague and I went with our hosts from the community to the local bar for some drinks. Our hosts ended up leaving and my colleague and I stayed later into the night. When we were ready to leave there were no taxis available, so we waited on the street with several other people for the next available cab. While we were waiting, a skirmish broke out beside us. Two Caucasian males in their late teens or early twenties were involved in a fight with a First Nations woman. The woman was quite large and was not intimidated by the young men who were taunting her and prodding her into the fight. At first we thought it was just an argument, but then the woman threw a punch, missed, and fell to the ground. The men took advantage of the situation and began punching her on the ground. Before my colleague and I could intervene, a group of people rushed in and initiated a series of physical and verbal jousts. The whole time, the two young men were laughing and making fun of this infuriated woman who was not backing down despite the shots she took. The angrier she got, the more they teased her and laughed at her. There were likely close to fifty people in the middle of the sidewalk pushing and shoving each other when a local police car slowly drove by but did not stop. The situation finally dissipated without involving the authorities and thankfully no one was seriously hurt. What was evident was that these two young men were preying on the woman's vulnerability, which speaks to the underlying racial tensions that exist at hockey tournaments as well as in daily life.

I was able to gain glimpses into these tensions through secondhand commentary as well as by observing firsthand how tournament participants were treated by non-First Nations people throughout the events. This is not to suggest that all or even the majority of host city or town residents acted disrespectfully or negatively towards First Nations tournament participants. What I did routinely observe, however, was a discrepancy between the way I was treated as a white man and the way my First Nations counterparts were treated. For example, during tournaments in the smaller towns, the restaurants would be packed with event participants. Very often my research assistants and I would be the only non-First Nations people in the restaurant. On countless occasions I would watch the servers curtly deal with their First Nations customers and then change their demeanor once they arrived at our table. There were even instances where the servers would subtly express relief to me after finishing with a First Nations table – either by rolling their eyes or through a sigh of frustration – and then initiate light banter. Similarly, in line at a confectionary store I would hear the cashier speak curtly to the First Nations customers ahead of me, but then become more congenial when serving me. I rarely spoke with the players about these issues, but one night, while out with some players and their girlfriends, a woman opened up to me about the racist treatment she endured living in the tournament town.

On this particular Sunday night, we went out after the team I was with lost in the championship game. I picked up two of the players and their girlfriends in my rental car and we went to the local bar to meet the rest of the team for one last night out before they all flew home. As I pulled up to the bar I began to park in front, but was told that I had better move the car to a safer place. The players had been to this bar the two previous nights, and based on what they had seen, I risked getting my windows smashed in if I parked right in front. They also joked about how rough the place was, saying that getting stabbed was not out of the realm of possibility. The mayhem of previous nights was not to be realized, however; the place was almost empty. Most teams and supporters had already gone home, so other than a few locals, the only people at the bar were players from the final two teams. We began ordering drinks, and as usual discussion focused on hockey: the day's loss, the tournament, tournaments past, and player exploits from years gone by. This was the first time, however, that I had sat and talked with not only players but also their girlfriends and wives, and as the night progressed conversations outside of hockey emerged. Two women in particular began talking about living in this town and the resentment they felt living under what they described as the spectre of racism. They explained that they dealt with racism daily, in both social and professional contexts. The joke about getting stabbed when we walked in was suddenly not so funny; they said whenever they went out they were always weary of a fight breaking out, which in some cases involved weapons. They said that as First Nations people they were looked down upon and treated unfairly. One woman explained to me that she confronted a supervisor at work about racist attitudes and it was an extremely difficult ordeal – she had avoided confrontation of this sort most of her life, but in this case was forced to take action because of the severity of the situation. She said it took tremendous courage for her to stand up to the injustice she faced, and most people she knew were too afraid to take similar action.

The sentiments expressed by these women were rarely heard from the players or tournament organizers, but my interactions with tournament attendees echoed many of these same concerns. There was one Elder who I had the pleasure of seeing at many of the events in western Canada. He had no direct involvement with any of the teams but would travel hours to watch the tournaments because of his love for hockey and the opportunity to visit with people he rarely got a chance to see. Whenever possible we would watch the games together. He was interested in the work I was doing and would ask me about what I was seeing so far. He would then offer his perspectives on First Nations hockey, but also on life in general. He explained to me early on that he was a recovering alcoholic and had suffered physical and mental abuse growing up. He said he talked openly about these things now, as this was part of the difficult and ongoing healing process. During one exchange he began describing how First Nations peoples feel that others perceive them as inferior and inadequate. He said the younger people from his nation are filled with dread and self-loathing and continue to turn to alcohol and drugs to cope with their struggles. Moreover, many people are scared to leave their communities and face the debasement and discrimination they expect to experience in urban centres, thus remaining ghettoized as individuals and as a people. I wrote the following in my field notes:

He then taps me on the shoulder and begins watching the game. We continue to talk off and on. He is a counsellor in his community. He wants people to move outside the 'box' he calls the reserve. Not so much abandon or move literally, but escape the insularity that is making it difficult to function outside of the reserve. Another thing is the fear people need to overcome. The whole perception and reduction of Aboriginal as something inferior: 'How they see us.'

His words were often filled with sadness and frustration, reminiscent of the two women who spoke to me about living in the tournament town. The demeaning and inferiorizing constructions of First Nations people provide the foundation for the racial tensions that subtly play out in everyday interactions, but are more visceral and volatile in late night drinking establishments. The story about Harry pummelling the Caucasian male and taunting him with 'Who's Hairy now?' was performed for comedic effect, yet at its core it is a retributive response to the inferiorized construction of First Nations people. It usurps – however temporarily – the power dynamic of white Western superiority and its spurning of the Other, and is punctuated wonderfully with 'Look who's laughing now.' The narrative is humorous because of the play on words, but also because of the inversion of power when Harry turns the white oppressor into the butt of his own joke. Through its telling and the realization of who *is* laughing now comes a collective empowerment, which adds to the story's success no matter how many times it's been told. But the story also highlights the racial tensions that First Nations people endure on a daily basis, which promote frustration, resentment, and occasional violence. Considering the frustration and resentment many First Nations people feel under this enduring spectre of racism, it makes me wonder not so much why violence occurs in these tournament towns, but why it doesn't happen more often.

Conclusion

Not including a section of violence in a book on First Nations hockey would be disingenuous, not because of the propensity of violence, but because of the persistent associations of violence with First Nations hockey. Through my extensive observation and participation in First Nations hockey over a three-year period it was evident that these violent associations were fallacious. The tournaments would be more accurately characterized as positive community gatherings celebrating the multitude of cultures and communities that attend the events. The hockey itself is relatively devoid of fighting or any other violent behaviour, and the stands were typically filled with men and women of all ages proudly cheering for their community teams. Incidents of violence that did occur during the tournaments were isolated events that were no more severe than the violence that occurs in Euro-Canadian hockey contexts. Yet there can be a darker side to these events, which I observed in late-night social activities where alcohol and other substance abuses were prevalent. All tournament organizers have made tremendous efforts to ensure the arena environments are devoid of alcohol – and in some cases even people who show signs of inebriation are not allowed in – but it is impossible to control or monitor what takes place outside of the arena grounds. What must be put into context, however, is that the vast majority of participants (whether players or spectators) are not involved in the violent or destructive behaviour I have described above. Not a single person I knew was actually involved in any violence, nor did they have any interest in participating in it. Participants who I came to know over this fieldwork saw themselves as vulnerable to unsolicited violence that stemmed primarily from racial tensions. This is not to say that Caucasians were primarily responsible for the violence or that it always directly involved non-Aboriginals. But the debasement of First Nations people and their culture has led to frustration, fear, and anger, which manifests itself in various ways. This could be through self-destructive behaviour such as substance abuse or suicide, or through violence against others. When violence does occur, perceptions of First Nations peoples as violent and dangerous are perpetuated, creating a self-fulfilling prophecy. As a result, incidents of violence and public disorder garner more attention by local media and community residents than the tournaments themselves, which are highly valuable cultural events.

The discrepancy between what is projected on First Nations hockey and what is actually occurring is significant also in that it brings us back to the theoretical foundation of this book, that is, the potential for First Nations hockey to evoke a type of border thinking within the larger modern Western world system. Here we see the construct of First Nations hockey as locally produced, but resulting from and in response to large global designs. The Euro-Canadian model of sport is adopted and transformed into meaningful cultural practices, yet is constrained by projections of what First Nations people, and in turn their sporting practices, are. It is what Mignolo refers to as 'mundialización and culture,' which are the 'local histories *in* which global designs are enacted or where they have to be adapted, adopted, transformed, and rearticulated. Both local histories are mediated by the structure of power – more specifically, by the coloniality of power that articulates the colonial differences between local histories projecting and exporting global designs and local histories importing and transforming them' (2000, 278). Unlike Mignolo, however, border thinking (gnosis) does not need articulation through an emergent formalized epistemological paradigm, but rather it is our role as academics to discover the sites of enunciation through daily cultural practices and lived experiences. In this sense one does not need to search for some remnant of traditional knowledge or spiritualism from a culture's past, but instead discover what he refers to as double consciousness through present-day articulations of self, culture, and identity. The final chapter intends to expose the meaningful articulations of First Nations hockey as a type or border thinking/gnosis or double consciousness that emerges through the cracks of dominant Western culture. Hockey becomes what the Elder referred to as 'moving outside of the box' and reclaiming space for the expression and affirmation of culture and identity.

5 Hockey as Border Thinking

In Rodolfo Kusch's ([1970] 2010) now-classic ethnographic work entitled *Indigenous and Popular Thinking in América*, the second chapter focuses on interactions between Kusch's research team and local villagers in rural Bolivia. Kusch describes how a grandfather and grandson responded to a suggestion to improve water extraction by taking advantage of an offer through the Agricultural Extension Office to get a free hydraulic water pump. Instead of reacting positively to the advice, the grandson, only 'to be agreeable, answered between clenched teeth: "Yes, we are going to go [to get the pump]"' (9). The grandfather refused to even respond to the suggestion and stood in relative silence staring out into the arid land. The seemingly innocuous suggestion made by Kusch's assistant and the unanticipated responses encapsulate what Kusch is aiming to expose: the misguided imposition of modernity and its reverence for technology and progress onto subjugated local knowledges and practices. His work is an attempt to resituate local knowledge in opposition to modernity's epistemological dominance and reveal the legitimacy of other ways of knowing. The scene exemplifies what Walter Mignolo (2000) calls 'the conflict between "indigenous" and "modern" knowledge. The conflict, in other words, is in the very fact of thinking that there is an "indigenous" knowledge opposed to "modern" forms of knowledges, in this case, actualized by technology' (301). This conflict is exposed through interactions between the researcher, vestibule of modern Western science and academia, and local inhabitants, who maintain their unique histories despite the enveloping trajectories of Western colonialism.

The notion of conflict resonated with me in my own research, as I too became exposed to the breakdown of the modern Western epistemic that continues to inform how I construct the world around me. In this final chapter I wish to celebrate points of disjuncture even further in hope of destabilizing the persistence of modern trajectories and exposing another way of thinking/being, or border gnosis. For those familiar with this concept and the group of scholars who work with it (see Escobar 2010), I am taking liberties with its meaning and general application. The term border gnosis has come to be a homology of indigenous knowledge and the act of articulating this knowledge within the grand scheme of decolonization. In 'Theorizing from the Borders' Mignolo and Tlostanova (2006) use 'border thinking' and 'theorizing' interchangeably (206), which is consistent with Mignolo's original (2000) conception of border gnoselogy and its distinction from gnosis. For Mignolo, the word gnosis means knowledge in general whereas gnoseology refers to 'the discourse about gnosis' (ibid., 11). Border gnoseology, then, 'is a critical reflection on knowledge production from both the interior borders of the modern/colonial world system . . . and its exterior borders' (ibid.). For Mignolo real border thinking occurs only when subaltern scholars formally articulate local knowledge, or engage in the act of gnoseology: 'In Spanish America true border thinking does not emerge until the work of José María Arguedas and Rigoberta Menchú' (ibid., 166). Arguedas and Menchú are people who grew up in a tribal Peruvian village and later acquired formal education, possessing what Dubois ([1903] 2007) and later Mignolo refer to as a double consciousness. Working from both local and Western epistemologies a critique of the latter is enabled, making way for alternative knowledges. While such critical deconstruction is important and, I would argue, necessary for tangible decolonizing strategies, the significance of border gnosis is not sufficiently appreciated. By exposing First Nations hockey as a type of border gnosis, I hope to provide direction for border gnoseology to unfold. This approach acts on Mignolo and Tlostanova's (2006, 211) premise of border thinking when they write: 'If border thinking is the unavoidable condition of imperial/colonial domination, *critical* border thinking is the imperial/ condition transformed into epistemic and political projects of decolonization' (emphasis added). By locating expressions of border gnosis in specific First Nations contexts, a new scholarship of critical border gnoseology can begin to shape the radical process of decolonization.

Stickhandling through Coloniality

Before discussing First Nations hockey as a type of border thinking, it is necessary to understand the conditions that make border thinking not only possible, but, as Mignolo and Tlostanova claim, inevitable (ibid., 211). Border thinking occurs as a result of living under the violence of coloniality, which is distinguished from colonialism: '[coloniality] refers to long-standing patterns of power that emerged as a result of colonialism, but that define culture, labor, intersubjective relations, and knowledge production well beyond the strict limits of colonial administration' (Maldonado-Torres 2010, 97). The distinction is of special significance when responding to parts of the world that have undergone formal stages of decolonization, where exchanges of power from colonial powers to the previously colonized have occurred. Quijano (2010) is correct in saying that 'direct, political, social and cultural domination . . . established by the Europeans . . . has been defeated in the large majority of the cases,' but that the 'specific structure of power' that 'produced specific social discriminations which were later codified as "racial", "ethnic", "anthropological" or "national" persist in both colonial and post-colonial societies' (22). First Nations peoples in Canada live under direct domination of the Canadian state and the subsequent power structures that have been codified into everyday existence. The doubling effect of colonization and coloniality means that as colonial subjects people 'breathe coloniality all the time and everyday' (Maldonado-Torres 2010, 97). It also effects double consciousness.

W.E.B. Du Bois was an African American social scientist, politician, and activist living in the northeastern United States in the late nineteenth and early twentieth century (Marable 1986). His work *The Souls of Black Folk*, originally published in 1904, is a groundbreaking critique of race relations in America. Much of his work was built around his own troubled experiences as a Black scholar and public official embroiled in the privileged world of predominantly white America yet painfully outside of the 'whitestream' (Denis 1997). He described this duality as a double consciousness that was informed by his own local cultural heritage and the larger dominant culture in which he lived. In an especially telling passage he writes, 'It is a peculiar sensation, this double-consciousness, this sense of always looking at one's self through the eyes of others, of measuring one's soul by the tape of a world that looks on in amused contempt and pity. One ever feels his twoness – an American, a Negro; two souls, two thoughts, two unreconciled strivings; two warring ideals in one dark body, whose dogged strength alone keeps it from being torn asunder' (8). These sentiments are echoed in other colonial contexts around the world. In the preface to Albert Memmi's *The Colonizer and the Colonized* (2003) he offers what he refers to as a confession for providing a portrait of the colonizer, the 'adversary': 'Here is a confession I have never made before: I know the colonizer from the inside almost as well as I know the colonized' (9). As a Jewish person living in colonial Tunisia in the first half of twentieth century, his writings emphasize the interdependence between the colonizer and the colonized through his experience existing betwixt and between these racialized political polarities. Later in his preface he writes, 'I was a sort of half-breed of colonization, understanding everyone because I belonged completely to no one' (ibid., 12).

Notions of double consciousness are being expressed by First Nations in Canada, most notably by Mi'kmaq Elder Albert Marshall whose thinking on the subject has been instrumental for the development of a science program at Cape Breton University based in both Western and traditional Mi'kmaq epistemologies (Hatcher et al. 2009). In an article co-authored by Marshall, the authors explain their concept of 'two-eyed seeing,' which refers to 'learning to see from one eye with the strengths of Indigenous ways of knowing and from the other eye with the strengths of Western ways of knowing and to using both of these eyes together' (146). Two-eyed seeing here is a conscious integrative effort, but the idea stems from Marshall's own two-eyed seeing that 'emerged in Atlantic Canada (the traditional territory of the Mi'kmaq Nation) because Mi'kmaq people are the Aboriginal people of North America who have had the longest experience of living side by side with the newcomers from Europe' (ibid.). Cape Breton University's integrative science program developed from this double consciousness evokes the possibility for critical border thinking and important first steps in decolonization. What separates the work of Mignolo and others from such integrative approaches, however, is that border thinking is not simply the accommodation of local ways of thinking/being within the larger colonial matrix, but a dismantling of dominant Western epistemologies caused as a result of the conflict between local and global perspectives, or the colonial difference. As such the risk of subsuming local ways of thinking and creating some form of epistemological hybridity is reduced. Border thinking is more akin to what Scollon and Scollon (1979) recognize as their own epistemological shortcomings working in remote First Nations contexts in Canada. In their ethnographic work in Fort Chipewyan, Alberta, they offer the term 'bush consciousness' to describe the incongruity between their own ways of thinking based in Western academia and Chipewyan experience-based epistemology. The term is not simply an acknowledgment of other ways of knowing, but rather an admission of their own limited consciousness, which is deficient in specific cultural contexts. Border thinking builds from this logic, which is not about accommodation, but rather

> integrating and superseding the restrictive logic behind the idea of 'civilization' by giving rise to what the civilizing mission suppressed: the self-appropriation of all the good qualities that were denied to the barbarians. 'Border thinking' in all its complexity . . . is a way of thinking that emerges as a response to the conditions of everyday life created by economic globalization and the new faces of the colonial difference. (2000, 303–4)

It is here then that we can begin examining First Nations hockey as a response to coloniality and as a critical site for the enunciation of border gnosis.

Hockey Pluriversality

In writing about specific features of First Nations hockey I am in no way attempting to essentialize qualities of First Nations hockey or culture, or to point to a type of difference that suggests or defines First Nations distinctiveness. In contrast, First Nations hockey provides a counter discourse to the grand narratives of modernity and the 'monoptic of abstract universals' that are somehow constructed to represent human experience (Mignolo 2000, 87). Modern sport continues to be a critical expression of modernity's grand narratives of progress, rationalization, individualism, leadership, and competition – all revered virtues of modern capitalism. The once local and multivarious physical pastimes of pre-modern societies were transformed into tools for inculcating young males with qualities to make them fit for serving nations and imperial empires (Guttmann 1994). This new sanitized construct of recreation, with its rules and regulations, has come to constitute 'sport' in the Western world. Modern sport demands participants conform to its rigid formulas, producing a singular sporting ethic with specific goals and outcomes expected as a result of participation (i.e., improved health and fitness, leadership skills, teamwork skills, competitive drive, and the creation of social networks). This understanding of sport has become a naturalized construct and part of the monoptic vision of modernity. Yet my experience participating in and observing hockey in First Nations contexts has destabilized the universality of sport, giving way to diverse and unexpected meanings. First Nations hockey is evidence of pluriversality (Mignolo and Tlostanova 2006), the multivarious constructs of sport that expose conflict with dominant practices and in turn expose the colonial difference. The fact that it is in the shape of the Euro-Canadian construct of sport is what enables border thinking, which

> structures itself on a double consciousness, a double critique operating on the imaginary of the modern/colonial world system, or modernity/coloniality. As such, it establishes alliances with the internal critique, the monoptic critique of modernity from the perspective of modernity itself . . . at the same time that it marks the irreducible difference of border thinking as a critique from the colonial difference. (Mignolo 2000, 87)

In my descriptions of encountering First Nations hockey in local communities and in tournament play, I have attempted to expose the conflict between local practices and my own sensibilities informed by Western/global imaginings of sport. Although my research was not an attempt to capture differences between First Nations and Euro-Canadian hockey, local particularities emerged along the way that fractured my previously monolithic readings of behaviour into multiple culture-specific meanings. My engagement in First Nations hockey activities destabilized my intimate and naturalized understanding of hockey and sport, exposing new ways of understanding the body and human interaction. This defamiliarization produced moments of tension or conflict, which I later recognized as points of enunciation of local meanings that I needed to accommodate in order to play.

These points of tension/conflict presented themselves in various ways, perhaps none as dramatic as when I was playing pick-up hockey in the remote community of Sandy Lake. At this point I had come to know many of the players quite well and I enjoyed playing with these friends in the weekly evening games. Pick-up hockey games were held each hour starting at about 8:00 p.m. The games were open to anyone willing to pay the five dollar participation fee, but certain time slots were associated with particular age groups and skill levels. In the short time I was in the community I managed to skate with most groups on various nights, but generally selected the time slot with the most players I knew. One evening, however, my student and I were invited to play with the more competitive group because they were short players. We did not know most of these players, but happily agreed to fill the empty spots.

Early in the game I noticed a large man on the ice was playing me quite aggressively, which was not typical in this recreational format (regardless of the skill level). When up against the boards this player would give me an extra shove or block me even though we were playing non-body-contact hockey. At times as I skated through open ice he skated in my path as if trying to knock me down, to the point that I felt it was getting slightly dangerous. He was the only player with this level of aggression and it was directed exclusively at me. The more I tried to ignore him, the more persistent he became. I interpreted his behaviour as some type of challenge beckoning a response. As the game continued I assumed that there was not much left for me to do but confront him, despite knowing that he would destroy me in any type of physical fight. By a certain point I just wanted it to end, and decided to pre-emptively strike him the next time he bore down on me. Soon, as I was chasing the puck in our end, he was directly on my tail pursuing me. I turned around to play the puck and cross-checked his upper body. Despite using as much force as possible, the contact had little physical effect on the player; instead, he skated into me and responded in a way that I could not have anticipated. He looked down at me and said, 'What the fuck was that for?' He appeared genuinely disturbed by my sudden and seemingly inappropriate outburst. He then simply carried on with the play as if nothing had happened, and for the remainder of the game did not concern himself with me. I was confused and suddenly embarrassed for misinterpreting his aggressive play as confrontational and uniquely directed at me. I likely will never know the player's thinking in playing me so aggressively from the outset of the game, but it was clearly not based in hostility or maliciousness. Perhaps he was simply enthusiastic about playing with someone from outside of the community, or this was just his style of play. Whatever the case, it was clear that I had misinterpreted his behaviour towards me.

Through this narrative I have tried to illustrate the multiplicity of meanings that are available in local expressions of hockey despite the appearance of standard Euro-Canadian play. Hockey was not simply played according to an assemblage of rules that maintain structural uniformity. Local values and meanings were imbued into each performance, which destabilized my own engagement in the activity. The basic elements of skating, passing, shooting, scoring, and checking remained constant, yet their execution and outcomes held varying significance. In each setting I found myself trying to negotiate my way through the game, regulating how much I should move the puck, how individually to play, how much effort to exude, how hard to check or not check, or, as in the example above, how to respond to other players on the ice. Such discrepancies in hockey experiences have been described by Collings and Condon (1996) in their seminal piece on Inuit physical recreational pursuits in Holman, Nunavut. They describe the disdain players from southern parts of Canada had for Inuit play, which did not align with typical Euro-Canadian hockey conventions:

> They frequently complain that Holman Inuit do not have well-developed skills and do not use teamwork to achieve what the Southerners assume to be the universal goal of hockey: putting the puck in the net. The game is often violent in a manner unfamiliar to these outsiders . . . A former recreation coordinator once complained that the problem with the way Inuit play hockey was that they 'weren't real men.' They relied on hitting people from behind and skating away (what Holman players call 'bothering') instead of dropping the gloves and fighting it out on the ice. (257)

What is important here is that what is being described is not merely a matter of variations in style of play, but the colliding of two different ways of knowing/being.

These local articulations of culture were often subtle and difficult to detect. They typically produced brief moments of tension during which I would temporarily feel out of place and would then need to re-negotiate myself back into the play. In the Esketemc First Nation, some of the older players would lightly chastise me for not scoring when I had the opportunity, despite there being no goalie and no defence. I thought playful passing and prolonging the play would be more welcomed than effortless scoring, yet to them this trivialized their game, producing the opposite to my intended effect. In addition to these subtle articulations, however, there were also more overt expressions of local culture that provide clear examples of border gnosis and the transformative potential of local practices that are entwined in global designs.

Toughness

In dispelling stereotypical formulations of First Nations hockey as excessively violent, it is important not to lose sight of meaningful associations with toughness that were evidenced in hockey play and comments from players and participants. In using the word 'toughness,' I am not referring to the masculinist constructions of toughness rightly critiqued in North American sport, 'in which the human body is routinely turned into a weapon to be used against other bodies, resulting in pain, serious injury, and even death' (Messner 1990, 204). Instead, First Nations constructions of toughness are grounded in qualities associated with perseverance, stoicism, and survival. Toughness manifested itself in a variety of ways during my research, but it was eloquently expressed in one conversation I had with an Elder while watching tournament play in Prince George. He described 'white people's' reactions to First Nations players who got hit hard but got right back up again. He said this impressed the white people he knew. I responded by saying how tough the First Nations' players were. He then said, 'Toughness is something we have learned from being Native. We have to do everything twice as hard as the white guy does to succeed.' He then pointed to the men playing on the ice and said, 'They need to simply grin and bear it. This is something we have learned from our grandmothers. They need to respect themselves and all else will be okay.' I found his comments striking in part because they speak to the resolve of First Nations people in the face of coloniality. Life is difficult for his people, and enduring oppression has required tremendous strength. But his comments were also striking because of who he assigns as the source of this power: the grandmother. Not only is this a dramatic departure from Western patriarchal constructs of power, but it is also illustrative of other ways of knowing, or border gnosis. Western constructs of power based in masculine conventions of objectivity, rationalism, and dominance are contrasted with the feminine construct of the grandmother whose cumulative experiences nurturing, protecting, and leading the communities are more meaningful articulations of strength and power. Interestingly, these qualities, which were not aligned with the physically dominant patriarchal construction typical in Euro-Canadian hockey, were made visible both on and off the ice.

I wish to draw on two examples to assist in making this point, one dealing with behaviour associated with tournament play, the other with more vernacular expressions of sport in a remote northern Ontario community. The first example refers back to the game described in Chapter 3 in Sioux Lookout, Ontario, where a team played without a full line-up. The team played hard, even after losing additional players over the course of the game. Though they ultimately lost, the players celebrated their efforts at the conclusion of the game with a group cheer at centre ice. What was lost on the scoreboard paled in comparison to what was won by playing through such difficult circumstances and not relenting until the final buzzer. The outcome was not as important as the process of playing, where players demonstrated valued toughness by playing through adversity. Playing through difficult circumstances became a recurrent theme throughout the tournaments and was manifested in a variety of ways.

The second example draws broadly from the many instances of First Nations players using old, worn-out, or substandard equipment that often put them at serious risk of injury. High-end hockey gear was certainly valued, as one player explained: 'I'm sure you probably noticed, most guys probably have Nike this or Nike that, Bauer. They don't have shitty equipment, because they take pride in being one of the better guys at the tournament.' This player was referring to the elite players in the tournament who played a high level of hockey and who generally had access to higher-quality gear. The relatively disadvantaged economic position of First Nations peoples in Canada, however, means that many players do not have the resources to spend between $500 and $600 on a pair of skates, or $200 on a hockey stick, and they are therefore forced to wear low-quality equipment that impedes protection and performance. Equipment shortcomings do not prevent players from participating, however, and in some cases this makeshift equipment is even worn like a badge of honour. I noted that various players would draw attention to their antiquated gear rather than trying to mask it. One player wore a hockey helmet from the 1970s that provided little to no protection. On the back of his head he pasted a fragile sticker, making fun of the fragility of his helmet but also the contents within. Other players wore regular eyeglasses without any face protection, compounding the risk of injury not simply from errant high sticks or pucks, but also from the damage the eyeglasses might cause coming into contact with the eye and nose area as a result of impact. I witnessed one player receive an open ice hit where his glasses were knocked off of his face and went flying in the air. As he was trying to pick himself up from the ice, he was also reaching for his glasses, which he could not see because of his impaired vision. He finally found them, picked himself up, and skated – grinning from ear to ear – towards his bench.

Playing hockey with inferior equipment points to the type of disadvantage the Elder was referring to when he said 'We have to do everything twice as hard as the white guy does to succeed.' For these players, playing despite limited resources is not new – I witnessed this firsthand watching youth play pick-up hockey in First Nations communities across the country. One of the most memorable of these experiences occurred in Sandy Lake, where I saw some boys and girls playing hockey on the frozen lake just below the 'hotel' where we were staying. It was about three o'clock in the afternoon, and the sun, along with the temperature, was starting to go down. My students and I grabbed our hockey sticks, bundled up in our warm winter clothes, and went down to see if we could play. The youth, ranging in ages from roughly six to ten, were thrilled to have us join them, and we played until dark on a five-by-three-metre clearing of ice. Some kids had skates (in one case at least two sizes too large), while others played in their boots. Beyond worn-down sticks that were generally too long for the kids, no other equipment was used. One boy did not have a stick, so his older brother would intermittently stop and let him use it. The younger boy would take a few shots, return the stick, and then go back to standing on the side watching the others play. Two snow chunks were used for a net at one end, and a broken piece of plywood at the other. The scene was like something out of Canadian popular culture (captured neatly, among others places, on the five dollar bill and in Tim Hortons television commercials[1]). In this game, however, kids were playing in torn winter jackets and jeans, some without hats or gloves. It was clear that some of them were cold as they blew on their raw red hands trying to keep warm in the −15° Celsius temperature. Despite this, the play was emphatic – kids proudly showed us their skills, risking nothing in the process. One player with a relatively strong shot fired the puck and hit a boy in the shin. The boy who had been hit winced briefly and wiped the snow from his oversized jeans, then continued on as though nothing had happened. I am not sure if I would have been as stoic upon receiving the same shot, and joked with him that I would have cried if I got hit that hard. Playing with these kids showed me firsthand where

---

1 Tim Hortons is a coffee and donut chain in Canada that often uses national themes and content, including hockey, in its television commercials.

this notion of toughness resides – there is nothing tougher than what they were displaying in front of me. This is how these kids learn to play hockey and, for many, it is what defines them as players. Toughness is a condition of existence, not a choice, and it is embodied in both formal and informal hockey experiences. It is not, however, based in male physical aggression or associated with dominance as in Euro-Canadian hockey. It is a way of being informed by local experience and knowledge, and as such is a form of border thinking. It also points to other ways of experiencing sport that transcend the dominant sport ethic, which should be even more evident in the next section, on competition.

Competition

Competition is one of the defining features of Western sport in that it serves to separate sport from other physical pursuits such as yoga, dance, and running (simply for the sake of exercise) (Coakley and Donnelly, 2009). In its earliest imaginings in the late 1800s and early 1900s, sport was based on aristocratic notions of fair play and gentlemanly conduct that attempted to diminish the importance of winning and losing. Modern sport's development alongside the rise of Western capitalism gradually produced specific meanings that were more aligned with progress, domination, and a win-at-all-cost approach to competition. This hyper-competitive sport model has been referred to as the dominant sport ethic, and continues to shape the sporting industry around the world through international sporting bodies like the International Olympic Committee, professional leagues and associations, the media complex that has been built around sport, and the sport manufacturing industry, including multinational corporations such as Nike. The pervasiveness of this dominant sport model has made it ripe for critique by globalization scholars, most notably in the area of the sociology of sport (Harvey, Rail, and Thibault 1996; Maguire 2004; Maguire 1999). Within this vast array of scholarship there have been those interested in the way local cultures have responded to these global forces and who ask if sport can be an expression of local culture just as much as it is evidence of globalization (Rowe 2003). What I am interested in, however, is not simply resistance to global or hegemonic designs, or evidence that a local exists, but rather alternative ways of knowing/being that expose cracks in the global/colonial imaginary. Border thinking is not resistance to the totalizing effects of coloniality; it is cultural articulations 'located at the intersection of local histories enacting global designs' (Mignolo 2000, 310) and effecting polyphonic epistemologies. Border thinking points to 'a world of multiple centers . . . dominated by none' (ibid.), which First Nations hockey exemplifies. The seemingly universal concept of competition is mediated through local specificities to enact multiple expressions.

Earlier I described the team who played under compromised conditions (with fewer players) and, through their unwillingness to capitulate to their opponents, took away a form of victory despite what the scoreboard read. Beyond exemplifying toughness and strength, this incident also speaks to the notion of competition and what it means to compete with one another, or in this case, with oneself. I witnessed one of the more vivid expressions of another way of knowing/being through competition at the conclusion of a game (described in Chapter 3) in which the on-ice official's error allowed one team to mount a comeback and eventually win. The losing team did not entirely share my outraged reaction to the game's outcome; despite the injustice, they were drawing tremendous satisfaction from the conflict that was now being extended through the postgame dispute of the other team's victory. One of the coaches explained, 'We always have this rivalry. We love it. We call them our cousins,' which completely undermined the outcome-oriented model of sport that I had grown up with. The players were still upset about losing, and the other team was jubilant in victory, but there was a double consciousness present where outcomes were valued but not overshadowed by the engagement itself. For these two communities, the opportunity to compete far exceeded any external gratification that winning might bring, and the postgame dispute simply extended the engagement. It was part of the competition that is infrequently afforded remote communities, who have limited opportunities to face external opponents. The fact that this dispute took place against their longtime rivals made it even more meaningful. This graciousness towards competition is a defining feature of this and many First Nations hockey tournaments, and an important part of what makes these events so appealing. Competition is not just a defining quality of sport in this context – it *is* sport.

The significance of competition was also made apparent when I played hockey with members of the Esketemc First Nation. My outcome-based vision of sport limited my ability, at least initially, to meaningfully participate. Over time I began to appreciate what was being asked of me, shed my self-conscious performativity, and simply play. My worries about 'showing-up' weaker players or seeming overzealous in any aspect of the game – skating, shooting, or simply effort – were gradually displaced by the satisfaction of simply engaging with my fellow players. There is a risk of romanticizing the experience, but it has little to do with connecting First Nations hockey practices with some pure or noble concept of sport associated with a golden age of the past. Rather, these expressions of sport are tied to the colonial experience and the legacy of suffering that this community, at least, has endured since European arrival. Community members live with the tragic legacy of alcohol and physical and sexual abuse every day, making hockey an incredible departure from ongoing suffering. This is not to suggest that hockey is a distraction; rather, it is a meaningful expression of self, a means of rediscovering the body, and as the former Chief of the Esketemc First Nation claimed, a vehicle for letting the First Nations spirit fly. It marks a radical departure from the suffering that the community endured for years and is now seeking to reconcile. Hockey incorporates the universal construct of sport, but its singular expression is fractured through the performance of new meanings, pointing to the colonial difference and the emergence of other ways of thinking/being. Through my participation in First Nations hockey I experienced the destabilizing effect of difference within a sport that I had known intimately for nearly forty years. Fragmentation of experience may be the most accurate depiction of what happened to me, and with it came liberation and the satisfaction of multiple ways of seeing. This, ultimately, is the essence of First Nations hockey – its non-essence, its pluriversality, its defiance of being one thing. It is also likely the reason it has tremendous value for First Nations peoples, whose engagement is reinvented to suit their own needs and purposes and as such continues to be a profound expression of local culture and identity.

Conclusion

In this chapter I have attempted to illustrate the ways in which local expressions of sport give way to a type of border thinking. I do not wish to give the impression that there are essential characteristics of First Nations hockey or that it is necessarily unique, but there are shared experiences that link First Nations peoples together in the face of coloniality and the structures of power that impact everyday existence for Aboriginal peoples. Understanding hockey's place within this context is just one avenue of an endless array of possibilities for border thinking in

response to the question: 'how do people in the world deal with Western economic, political and epistemic expansion if they do not want to
assimilate but choose to imagine a future that is their own invention
and not the invention of the empire, hegemonic or subaltern?' (Mignolo
and Tlostanova 2006, 209). As if in response to his own question, Walter
Mignolo has said:

> Since we cannot go back to other 'original' thinking traditions . . . because
> of the growing hegemony of the Western and modern/colonial world,
> what remains available to us is either reproducing Western abstract uni-
> versals and projecting them all over the world, or exploring the possibili-
> ties of border thinking to imagine possible futures. (Delgado, Romero, and
> Mignolo 2000, 11)

The intention of this project has been to understand if and how First
Nations hockey contributes to this process of destabilizing the global
imaginary and contributing to the reformulations of local knowledge/
ways of being in the cracks of the global imaginary. I unexpectedly experienced these ruptures myself as I began engaging in First Nations
hockey as a participant and observer. The difficulties I faced trying
to make sense of the experiences I encountered pointed to my own
monoptic vision and the necessity to engage in what Mignolo (2000)
refers to as 'pluritopic hermeneutics.' He explains, 'colonial semiosis
requires a pluritopic heremenuetics since in the conflict, in the cracks
and fissure where the conflict originates, a description of one side of
the epistemological divide won't do . . . because while the first problem
was to look into the spaces in between, the second was how to produce
knowledge from such in between spaces' (17–18). In other words, it is
not enough to point to the colonial difference, or the ruptures and con-
flicts that First Nations hockey exposes; it is necessary to also expose
the alternative, emergent epistemologies that are enacted in each performance. The potential of these emerging epistemologies for achieving meaningful steps towards decolonization remains to be seen, but
at the very least they point to gross deficiencies in a world structured
by the modern Western colonial imaginary. In its multiplicity, First Nations hockey aspires to what Mignolo believes possible through border
thinking – recognizing 'diversity as a universal project [which] allows
us to imagine alternatives to universalism' (2000, 310).

Conclusion

It has been nearly ten years since I began the research for this book, during which time I have shared in unforgettable experiences. The work opened my eyes to the incredible diversity of First Nations cultures and their interactions with the sport of hockey. The first research grant application I wrote for this project was rejected by the reviewers, primarily because they did not believe it would be possible for me to get the necessary access. Fortunately, a follow-up application was successful, and the project actually brought me closer to this research community than any I have ever worked with. This project was designed to take place within the public spaces of tournaments, but the people I met transformed the project by eagerly sharing with me their cultures and traditions that extended well beyond the realm of hockey. In the Esketemc First Nation, on my first night in the community, I was taken to an event where women were preparing Christmas crafts for an upcoming flea market. Without hesitation, the women brought us to their tables and prompted us to assist them in making the crafts. In Sandy Lake, in addition to playing hockey, community members took us ice fishing on numerous occasions to allow us to experience their environment and the cultural practices that are tied to the land. We spent full days on the frozen river with individuals and their families, but also sharing in the larger communal experience. Many people go ice fishing on weekends to gather food and socialize in northern Ontario's beautiful winter landscape. These are just two examples of the warm hospitality we were shown from people who proudly let us into their lives and shared their valued community customs.

The close relationships I was able to form were made possible because of people's love for hockey. My academic peers' astute reservations about my subject position as a non-Aboriginal researcher conducting research on First Nations populations became a non-issue when people heard I was doing research on hockey. Once they learned about the study, people who I met at the tournaments began inviting me into their communities. Many of the participants were quick to point out that Aboriginal people have been 'researched to death,' yet somehow when it came to hockey people had no shortage of things to say. They were also keen to have something produced on First Nations hockey. People would ask me for film footage from the tournaments, as my students or I recorded all of the tournament play. I made DVDs for a number of people so they could see themselves or games they watched as fans. Unlike most research I have conducted, where I repeatedly assured participants that their anonymity would be maintained, participants in this study were requesting to be mentioned in the book. People saw the work I was doing as showcasing their sport, and they wanted to be associated with it. As a result of this admiration for the project and desire to have First Nations hockey properly showcased, pressure mounted for me to write a book that satisfied these demands. I had become so close to people that I was feeling increasingly obligated to write something that they wanted rather than a critically informed piece suitable for an academic audience. Ironically, rather than a lack of access, it was the close relationships with participants that posed the greatest challenge to this study by making it difficult for me to write critically. I have struggled throughout the research trying to maintain academic and ethnographic integrity by speaking critically whenever necessary and avoiding writing what Greenhill (2000) has referred to as an 'ethnography of niceness.' Those doing ethnographic research work hard to build rapport and trust in order to gain intimate access to local behaviours and perspectives. In many cases, such as my own, this trust enables researchers to gain access to undesirable and often damaging behaviours that are worthy of commentary, but at what cost? I contend that with trust comes responsibility, and one must not jeopardize this relationship for the sake of ethnographic 'objectivity' – if such a thing even exists. How does one report, as objectively as possible, what is observed and experienced during the fieldwork, yet avoid breaking the trust that enabled the work to exist in the first place? Could my work have been more critical of the destructive behaviours (e.g., substance abuse and alcohol-related violence) that sometimes exist in tournament settings? Should I have taken issue with the highly gendered realities of First Nations hockey, and sport in general? Could I have pointed to the controversial decision made by some band councils to provide significant funds for hockey teams to participate in tournaments when communities are ravaged by disproportionately high levels of poverty, chronic disease, and myriad other social, economic, and health issues? Perhaps, but I would have compromised my position as a researcher and the relationships I have built over these past years. These constraints that I faced in writing the book must be conveyed to the reader.

In the end, I have attempted to balance fieldwork descriptions with theoretical perspectives to gain a deeper appreciation for what might otherwise simply be seen as hockey. I do not pretend to imagine that the perspectives I am offering are consistent with the thoughts of those involved in the sport, yet I have asked some of the participants to read the work and provide their feedback. This feedback was important for verifying the accuracy of tournament and community hockey descriptions, but also for questioning (not confirming) the various interpretations I have made throughout. The work is intended to prompt discussion and debate in hope of rethinking local cultural practices in the face of modern Western influence. In short, I am responding to Victoria Paraschak's (1997) important question: when 'marginalized groups find themselves in control of the construction of social practices, why do some continue to reproduce structures and/or activities of the dominant group, while others construct social practices which look quite different?' (2). This study suggests that it is through engagement in dominant structures that distinctive meanings and knowledges are produced. In other words, dominant structures are not being reproduced, they are being reconfigured, or, as Bhabha describes, people are redefining the signifying relations of signs. The reference to semiotics is apt in that hockey, as signifier, remains constant, yet the signified is remarkably distinctive as I demonstrated by pointing to the local meanings articulated in each hockey performance. The relationship between the signifier and signified is akin to what we have described as double consciousness, whereby dominant structures are infused with local meanings thus transforming the sign. This transformation gives way to border thinking and the destabilization of the coloniality of power.

I see this book's contribution in its ability to call attention to the variety of local cultural expressions imbued in a seemingly stable series of signs. Under the coloniality of power, First Nations peoples have been problematized in terms of health (e.g., obesity, type 2 diabetes), poverty, suicide rates, housing, drinking water, land claims – the list goes on. Not wishing to dispute the deplorable conditions in which many First Nations peoples in Canada live, and the gross disparities in nearly all socio-economic and health categories between First Nations peoples and the rest of Canada, these features hardly define who First Nations peoples are. These disparaging discourses contribute to Euro-Canadian monoptics of First Nations peoples as a problem that needs remedying, and this construction filters into everyday practices including sport. First Nations hockey is stigmatized as an excessively violent and dangerous site where social problems such as alcohol consumption and violence are exacerbated. When an incident of violence occurs at a game or a tournament, it reinforces this monoptic vision, further perpetuating the 'First Nations problem.' Yet this study has shown that First Nations hockey is as diverse as the peoples who play it. It can be violent just as it can be spiritual. It can be an opportunity for intense socialization and alcohol or narcotics usage, and it can also be a vehicle for sobriety. The only constant within its pluriversality is the process of investing local meanings within the vessel of hockey, reinventing it to suit local needs and interests. As such, performing hockey is a highly valued and meaningful expression of culture. Better yet, it is a locally contrived and fractious experience therefore exposing the gross deficiencies of a singular and inferiorizing vision of First Nations people. Through its expression it points to new ways of seeing First Nations culture and produces new ways of thinking about sport. The decolonization of knowledge is not simply recognizing marginal subaltern perspectives, but illuminating the reductionist impact the modern Western imaginary has on all human experience. The diversity of First Nations hockey experiences suggests other ways of knowing/being, and the emancipatory potential of border thinking. It is an expression of difference in the face of the dominant structures of power.

In uncovering this diversity of experience I hope to create impetus for celebrating First Nations hockey and making it visible to larger Canadian society. Observing and participating in hockey played in First Nations contexts awoke in me an awareness of the greater potential of hockey and sport in general. It forced me to think about hockey differently, both through my own physical engagement with the sport and through my understanding of the meanings associated with competition, teams, winning, or the idea of play itself. Whether it is in the context of high-performance tournaments or local vernacular expressions of hockey, each performance conveys culturally specific meanings and values. This was articulated most clearly by one player who described First Nations tournaments as an awakening. He played twelve seasons in the National Hockey League, eleven years in professional leagues in Europe, and two years playing for Canada's national team. By the time he retired he was sick of hockey. But when he was invited to play in a First Nations tournament, his involvement carried with it a new significance and he once again found himself excited by the sport. He explained it as follows:

> Yep, I don't miss the game at all. I mean it takes a lot for me to get out; it actually takes a lot for me to actually go play a game because I've had so many games from what, five years old? I was at the rink almost every day through the winter, to the rink and back. I mean learning how to skate; I was out there every day for hours and hours and hours. I did that until I was thirty-nine, and so when I talk to kids I say, to become a success, you know, here's how much time it's gonna take. Look at my life, at thirty-nine years old, I can honestly say that thirty to thirty-one of those years, I was on the ice every day. And not having to do that anymore was one of the reasons I quit. I mean, I was getting absolutely sick of putting my equipment on, of having to go practice, of having to go – the games themselves I loved. When I was on the ice I loved it, but to get dressed and actually get out there was tough. Now that I've quit, I don't miss the game itself. I miss the friends, I miss the dressing room, I miss the competition, but I don't miss the actual act of playing hockey. But when I get to the tournaments, and I'm not at home, it's easy, because that's what I'm there for. And it's fun, I get to see, like I said, I've never played, I haven't played in very many Aboriginal tournaments, so it's fun for me to reintroduce myself to the community that way, where they remember me from playing in Montreal, Pittsburgh, and Detroit, and wonder where I've been. It's like, 'nobody knew where you were,' and now they know I've been in Europe, and I reintroduce myself that way . . . I want to go out there for the next couple years I think I'll represent myself that way, and after that I'll probably play less and less. I'll play in the old-timers, I'll go out there for a little swag, but I can still represent myself half-decently, that's important to me, because that's how I remember myself playing.

Playing hockey in the best leagues in the world with the best players eventually became banal for this man, to the point that he wanted to discontinue playing altogether. The invitation to play in a First Nations hockey tournament exposed him to new meanings of the sport and made it something highly personal. He is now one of the leading ambassadors for First Nations hockey. He inspires young players across the country by visiting reserve communities, putting on hockey clinics, and simply sharing his positive approach to life. His energy is contagious – people feel better around him. These are the hockey experiences that need to be shared and celebrated to begin fracturing the oppressive narratives of what it means to be First Nations in Canada.

Hockey in First Nations communities, then, must be understood as having profound significance. In taking up the sport First Nations peoples are exposing the colonial difference. They disrupt the rigid structures and meanings of modern sport, pointing to the disjuncture between modern trajectories and the local epistemologies embroiled in these overarching Western constructs. The signifier (in this case hockey, but it could be any other cultural practice) is transformed through local engagement, exposing new meanings and new potential for sport. This process of engagement is merely one example of the endless interactions of local and global trajectories. Everyday existence is in some form a negotiation of the lived reality of coloniality where First Nations peoples engage with the dominant structures of power. Whether it be attending school under provincial ministries, gaining employment in a Western capitalist-driven economy, or seeking medical service in clinics and hospitals, First Nations peoples negotiate their way through the lived reality of coloniality. The tensions that are embedded in these negotiations point to the colonial difference, but also to news areas of local enunciation. Hockey is a particularly important site of enunciation because of its prominence as a national symbol of Canadian identity. The passion First Nations peoples have for the sport leads to its embrace and its dismantling through diverse acts of engagement. Hockey passion fuels its consumption, and, in turn, its proliferation, but never as a mere reproduction of dominant forms. First Nations hockey reconstitutes dominant forms in diverse local contexts, which ultimately points to its value within the larger project of decolonization.

I set out in this research to document local expressions of sport. I could not have anticipated the profound effect it would have on me as an individual and as a researcher. The project exposed alternative ways of understanding sport and the endless array of meanings that are manifested through each localized performance. It also exposed First Nations peoples' active engagement with the coloniality of power through new paths of resistance and transformation. This work has fostered my involvement in new areas of local expression, primarily as they relate to land-based activities in remote northern First Nations communities. Understanding sport in First Nations communities has pointed to other ways of knowing that I continue to apply to my current research on local food practices and the relationship between the land and community health. The close relationships that I established with the participants in this study were instrumental in making me recognize the need for community collaboration and partnership in all my research. First Nations hockey illuminates other ways of being/knowing that challenge how researchers understand behaviour and how Western constructs of knowledge are grossly inadequate. For this reason it is not enough to simply identify other ways of being through sport; it is important to elucidate how First Nations hockey and other local cultural practices offer alternatives to the monoptic vision of modernity. First Nations hockey is a celebration of diversity and heterogeneity in the face of global homogeneity. It exposes cracks within the global imaginary and new loci for enunciation and meaning making. It is in essence a recognition of border gnosis, paving the way for new areas of critical articulation from the borders and the ultimate objective of border gnoseology. How I as a Euro-Canadian scholar can contribute to this subaltern theorizing remains to be seen, but it informs how I have done and continue to do research. It provides incentive and direction for a new epistemological research paradigm that points to the challenges for those working with indigenous populations. In taking up this challenge my goal is to promote a new space for alternative ways of knowing within Western epistemology, and rightfully offer critical steps for the larger project of decolonization.

References

Allinger, T.L., and A.J. Van Den Bogert. 1997. Skating technique for the straights, based on the optimization of a simulation model. *Medicine and Science in Sports and Exercise* 29 (2):279–86.

Bhabha, H. 1991. 'Race', time and the revision of modernity. *The Oxford Literary Review* 13 (1–2):193–219.

Birrell, S. 1989. Racial relations theories and sport: Suggestions for a more critical analysis. *Sociology of Sport Journal* 6 (3):212–27.

Bloom, J. 2000. *To Show What an Indian Can Do: Sports at Native American Boarding Schools*. Vol. 2, *Sport and Culture Series*. Minneapolis: University of Minnesota Press.

Bopp, M., J. Bopp, and P. Lane. 1998. 'Community Healing and Aboriginal Social Security Reform: A Study Prepared for the Assembly of First Nations Aboriginal Social Security Reform Strategic Initiative.' http://www.4worlds.org/4w/ssr/pageone.html.

Bourdieu, P. 1988. Program for a sociology of sport. *Sociology of Sport Journal* 5 (2):153–61.

Bugmann, M. 2008. *Savage to Saint: The Karl May Story*. New York: BookSurge Publishing.

Burstyn, V. 1999. *The Rites of Men: Manhood, Politics, and the Culture of Sport*. Toronto: University of Toronto Press.

Carrington, B. 1998. Sport, masculinity, and black cultural resistance. *Journal of Sport and Social Issues* 22 (3):275–98.

Castellano, T., and I. Soderstrom. 1992. Therapeutic wilderness programs and juvenile recidivism: A program evaluation. *Journal of Offender Rehabilitation* 17 (3/4):19–46.

City of Greater Sudbury. 2002. 'Little NHL hockey tournament returns to Greater Sudbury,' October 24. http://www.grandsudbury.ca/pubapps/newsreleases/index.cfm?Release_id=523&lang=ko.

Coakley, J. 1994. *Sport in Society: Issues and Controversies*. 5th ed. St Louis: Mosby.

Collings, P., and R.G. Condon. 1996. Blood on the ice: Status, self-esteem, and ritual injury among Inuit hockey players. *Human Organization* 55 (3):253–9.

Davis, L. 1993. Protest against the use of Native American mascots: A challenge to traditional American identity. *Journal of Sport Issues* 17 (1):9–22.

Delgado, L.E., R.J. Romero, and W. Mignolo. 2000. Local histories and global designs: An interview with Walter Mignolo. *Discourse* 22 (3):7–33.

Deloria, P.J. 2004. *Indians in Unexpected Places*. Lawrence: University of Kansas Press.

Deloria, V. 1978. Civilization and isolation. *The North American Review* 263 (2):11–14.

Denis, J.C. 1997. *We Are Not You: First Nations and Canadian Modernity*. Peterborough, ON: Broadview Press.

Diaz, V. 2010. *Repositioning the Missionary: Rewriting the Histories of Colonialism, Native Catholicism, and Indigeneity in Guam*. Honolulu: University of Hawai'i Press.

Dubois, W.E.B. (1903) 2007. *The Souls of Black Folk*. Oxford: Oxford University Press.

Dunning, E., ed. 1971. *The Sociology of Sport*. London: F. Cass.

Dussel, E. 1995. *The Invention of the Americas: Eclipse of 'The Other' and the Myth of Modernity*. Translated by M.D. Barber. New York: Continuum.

Ekholm-Friedman, K., and J. Friedman. 1995. Global complexity and the simplicity of everyday life. In *Worlds Apart: Modernity through the Prism of the Local*, edited by D. Miller. New York: Routledge.

Escobar, A. 2010. Worlds and knowledges otherwise: The Latin American modernity/coloniality research program. In *Globalization and the Decolonial Option*, edited by W.D. Mignolo and E. Escobar. New York: Routledge.

Fisher, D.M. 2002. *Lacrosse: A History of the Game*. Baltimore: The Johns Hopkins University Press.

Forsyth, J., and M. Heine. 2008. Sites of meaning, meaningful sites? Sport and recreation for Aboriginal youth in inner city Winnipeg, Manitoba. *Native Studies Review* 17 (2):99–113.

Forsyth, J., and K.B. Wamsley. 2006. 'Native to Native . . . we'll recapture our spirits': The world Indigenous Nations Games and North American Indigenous Games as cultural resistance. *The International Journal of the History of Sport* 23 (2):294–314.

Foucault, M. 1977. *Discipline and Punish: The Birth of the Prison*. Great Britain: Penguin Books.

Fournier, S., and E. Crey. 1997. *Stolen from Our Embrace: The Abduction of First Nations Children and the Restoration of Aboriginal Communities*. Vancouver: Douglas & McIntyre.

Franks, R. 1982. *What's in a Nickname: Exploring the Jungle of College Athletic Mascots*. Amarillo: Ray Franks Publishing.

Furniss, E.M. 1987. 'A Sobriety Movement Among the Shuswap Indians of Alkali Lake.' MA thesis, University of Victoria, http://hdl.handle.net/2429/26816.

Gems, G. 2006. *The Athletic Crusade: Sport and American Cultural Imperialism*. Lincoln: University of Nebraska Press.

Grant, G. 1986. *Technology & Justice*. Concord, ON: House of Anansi Press Limited.

Greenhill, P. 2002. Folk and academic racism: Concepts from Morris and folklore. *Journal of American Folklore* 115 (456):226–46.

Gruneau, R. 1993. The critique of sport in modernity: Theorising power, culture, and the politics of the body. In *The Sports Process: A Comparative and Developmental Approach*, edited by E.G. Dunning, J.A. Maguire, and R.E. Pearton. Windsor, ON: Human Kinetics.

Guay, D. 1989. Les origines du hockey. *Canadian Journal of History of Sport* 20 (1):32–46.

Guggenheim, J.A. 1998. The Indians' Chief Problem: Chief Wahoo as state sponsored discrimination and a disparaging mark. *Cleveland State Law Review* 46 (2):211–37.

Guttmann, A. 1978. *From Ritual to Record*. New York: Columbia University Press.

———. 1994. *Games and Empires: Modern Sports and Cultural Imperialism*. New York: Columbia University Press.

Habermas, J. 1984. *The Theory of Communicative Action*. Vol. 1. Boston: Beacon Press.

Hallinan, C., and B. Judd. 2009. Race relations, Indigenous Australia and the social impact of professional Australian Football. *Sport in Society* 12 (9):1220–35.

Hargreaves, J. 1986. *Sport, Power, and Culture: A Social and Historical Analysis of Popular Sports in Britain*. New York: St. Martin's.

———, ed. 1982. *Sport, Culture, and Ideology*. London: Routledge & Kegan Paul.

Hartmann, D. 2000. Rethinking the relationships between sport and race in American culture: Golden ghettos and contested terrain. *Sociology of Sport Journal* 17 (3):229–53.

Harvey, J. 1988. Sport policy and the welfare state: An outline of the Canadian case. *Sociology of Sport Journal* 5 (4):315–29.

Harvey, J., G. Rail, and L. Thibault. 1996. Globalization and sport: Sketching a theoretical model for empirical analysis. *Journal of Sport & Social Issues* 20 (3):258–77.

Hatcher, A., C. Bartlett, A. Marshall, and M. Marshall. 2009. Two-eyed seeing in the classroom environment: Concepts, approaches, and challenges. *Canadian Journal of Science, Mathematics and Technology Education* 9 (3):141–53.

Hazlehurst, K. 1994. *A Healing Place: Indigenous Visions for Personal Empowerment and Community Recovery*. Rockhampton, Qld., Australia: Central Queensland University Press.

Heine, M. 2006. *Inuit Games: An Instruction and Resource Manual*. Yellowknife, NWT: Sport North Federation.

Henry, L. 1996. 'Where hockey meets powwow.' *Wawatay Online News*, http://www.wawatay.on.ca/index.php?module=pagesetter&func=viewpub&tid=1&pid=497.

Hokowhitu, B. 2009. Māori rugby and subversion: Creativity, domestication, oppression and decolonization. *International Journal of the History of Sport* 26 (16):2314–34.

Indian and Northern Affairs Canada. 1996. *Report of the Royal Commission on Aboriginal Peoples*. Ottawa: Government of Canada.

Iso-Ahola, S.E., and E.D. Crowley. 1991. Adolescent substance abuse and leisure boredom. *Journal of Leisure Research* 23 (3):260–71.

James, C.L.R. 1963a. *Beyond a Boundary*. New York: Pantheon Books.

———. 1963b. *The Black Jacobins: Toussaint l'ouverture and the San Domingo Revolution*. New York: Vintage Books.

———. 1969. *A History of Negro Revolt*. New York: Haskell House Publishers.

Judd, B.A., and C. Hallinan. 2007. Blackfellas basketball: Aboriginal identity and Anglo-Australian race relations in regional basketball. *Sociology of Sport Journal* 24 (4):421–36.

Kasson, J.S. 2000. *Buffalo Bill's Wild West: Celebrity, Memory, and Popular History*. New York: Hill and Wang.

King, C.R., and C.F. Springwood. 2001. *Team Spirits: The Native American Mascots Controversy*. Lincoln: University of Nebraska Press.

King, N. 2001. C.L.R. *James and Creolization: Circles of Influence*. Jackson, MS: University Press of Mississippi.

Kusch, R. (1970) 2010. *Indigenous and Popular Thinking in América*. Translated by M. Lugones and J.M. Price. Durham, NC: Duke University Press.

LeCompte, M.D., and J.J. Schensul. 1999. *Analyzing & Interpreting Ethnographic Data*. Walnut Creek, CA: AltaMira Press.

Long, N. 2000. Exploring local/global transformations: A view from anthropology. In *Anthropology, Development and Modernities: Exploring Discourses, Counter-Tendencies and Violence*, edited by A. Arce and N. Long. New York: Routledge.

Maguire, J. 1999. *Global Sport: Identities, Societies, Civilizations*. Cambridge: Polity.

Maguire, J.A. 2004. Globalisation and the making of modern sport. *Sportwissenschaft* 34 (1):7–20.

Maldonado-Torres, N. 2010. On the coloniality of being: Contributions to the development of a concept. In *Globalization and the Decolonial Option*, edited by W. Mignolo and A. Escobar. New York: Routledge.

Marable, M. 1986. *W.E.B. DuBois: Black Radical Democrat*. Vol. 3. Boston: Twayne.

Martin, L.H. 1988. *Technologies of the Self: A Seminar with Michel Foucault*. London: Tavistock.

Mason, C.W. 2008. The construction of Banff as a 'natural' environment: Sporting festivals, tourism and representations of Aboriginal Peoples. *Journal of Sport History* 35 (2):221–39.

———. 2009. The Buffalo Nations/Luxton Museum: Tourism, regional forces and problematizing cultural representations of Aboriginal Peoples in Banff, Canada. *International Journal of Heritage Studies* 15 (4):351–69.

———. 2010. Consuming the physical and cultural practices of Aboriginal Peoples: Spaces of exchange, conflict and (post)colonial power relations. In *Sport and Identity*, edited by J. Hughson. London: Edwin Mellen Press.

McCann, R., and C.D. Peters. 1996. At-risk youth: The Phoenix phenomenon. *Journal of Physical Education, Recreation, and Dance* 67 (2):38–40.

McDevitt, P. 2004. *May the Best Man Win: Sport, Masculinity, and Nationalism in Great Britain and the Empire, 1880–1935*. New York: Palgrave Macmillan.

Memmi, A. 2003. *The Colonizer and the Colonized*. 4th ed. London: Earthscan Ltd.

Messner, M. 1990. When bodies are weapons: Masculinity and violence in sport. *International Review for the Sociology of Sport* 25 (3):203–20.

Mignolo, W.D. 1993. Colonial and postcolonial discourse: Cultural critique or academic colonialism? *Latin American Research Review* 28 (3):120–34.

———. 2000. *Local Histories/Global Designs: Coloniality, Subaltern Knowledges, and Border Thinking*. Princeton, NJ: Princeton University Press.

Mignolo, W.D., and M.V. Tlostanova. 2006. Theorizing from the borders: Shifting to geo-and body-politics of knowledge. *European Journal of Social Theory* 9 (2):205–21.

Miller, J.R. 2000. *Skyscrapers Hide the Heavens: A History of Indian-White Relations in Canada*. 3rd ed. Toronto: University of Toronto Press.

Moses, L.G. 1996. *Wild West Shows and the Images of American Indians, 1883–1933*. Albuquerque: University of New Mexico Press.

Mudimbe, V. 1988. *The Invention of Africa: Gnosis, Philosophy, and the Order of Knowledge*. Bloomington: Indiana University Press.

Oxendine, J. 1988. *American Indian Sports Heritage*. Champaign, IL: Human Kinetics Books.

Palmer, A. 2005. *Maps of Experience: The Anchoring of Land to Story in Secwepemc Discourse*. Toronto: University of Toronto Press.

Paraschak, V. 1995. The Native sport and recreation program, 1972–1981: Patterns of resistance, patterns of reproduction. *Canadian Journal of History of Sport* 26 (2):1–18.

———. 1997. Variations in race relations: Sporting events for Native Peoples in Canada. *Sociology of Sport Journal* 14 (1):1–21.

———. 1998. 'Reasonable amusements': Connecting the strands of physical culture in Native lives. *Sport History Review* 29:121–31.

Perrot, N. 1973. *Mémoire sur les Moeurs, Coustumes, er Relligion des Sauvages de l'Amérque Septentrionale*. Edited by J. Tailhan. Montréal: Éditions Élysée.

Peters, J. 2003. 'D-man hanging up his Lumber King jersey.' *Prince George Citizen*, 12 April 2003.

Pewewardy, C.D. 1991. Native American mascots and imagery: The struggle of unlearning Indian stereotypes. *Journal of Navajo Education* 9 (1):19–23.

Place, H. 1999. *Dog Creek: A Place in the Cariboo*. Surrey, BC: Heritage House Publishing Co.

Powers-Beck, J. 2004. *The American Indian Integration of Baseball*. Lincoln: University of Nebraska Press.

Pratt, M.L. 2002. Modernity and periphery: Toward a global and relational analysis. In *Beyond Dichotomies: Histories, Identities, Cultures, and the Challenge of Globalization*, edited by E. Mudimbe-Boyi. Albany, NY: State University of New York Press.

Preuss, H. 2004. *The Economics of Staging the Olympics: A Comparison of the Games, 1972–2008*. Cheltenham, UK: Edward Elgar Publishing Limited.

Quijano, A. 1997. 'The colonial nature of power and Latin America's cultural experience.' Paper presented at the ISA Regional Conference, Sociology in Latin America, Colonia Tovar, Venezuela, July 7–9.

———. 2010. Coloniality and modernity/rationality. In *Globalization and the Decolonial Option*, edited by W. Mignolo and A. Escobar. New York: Routledge.

Rail, G., and J. Harvey. 1995. Body at work: Michel Foucault and the sociology of sport. *Sociology of Sport Journal* 12 (2):164–79.

Ribeiro, D. 1968. *The Civilizational Process*. Washington: Smithsonian Institution Press.

Robidoux, M.A. 2001. *Men at Play: A Working Understanding of Professional Hockey*. Montreal, QC: McGill-Queen's University Press.

———. 2002. Imagining a Canadian identity through sport: A historical interpretation of lacrosse and hockey. *Journal of American Folklore* 115 (456):209–25.

———. 2004. Narratives of race relations in southern Alberta: An examination of conflicting sporting practices. *Sociology of Sport Journal* 21 (3):281–301.

Robidoux, M.A., and P. Trudel. 2006. Hockey Canada and the bodychecking debate in minor hockey. In *Artificial Ice: Hockey, Culture and Commerce*, edited by D. Whitson and R. Gruneau. Peterborough, ON: Broadview Press.

Rowe, D. 2003. Sport and the repudiation of the global. *International Review for the Sociology of Sport* 38 (3):281–94.

Saggers, S., and D. Gray. 1998. *Dealing with Alcohol: Indigenous Usage in Australia, New Zealand and Canada*. Cambridge, UK: Cambridge University Press.

Said, E. 1993. *Culture and Imperialism*. New York: Vintage Books.

———. 1994. *Orientalism*. New York: Vintage Books.

Saskatchewan Indian. 'Hockey Night in North Battleford.' March 1972, http://www.sicc.sk.ca/iframe-test.html.

Scollon, R., and S.B.K. Scollon. 1979. *Linguistic Convergence: An Ethnography of Speaking at Fort Chipewyan, Alberta*. London: Academic Press.

Shogan, D. 1999. *The Making of High-Performance Athletes: Discipline, Diversity, and Ethics*. Toronto, ON: University of Toronto Press.

Sigelman, L. 1998. Hail to the Redskins? Public reactions to a racially insensitive team name. *Sociology of Sport Journal* 15 (4):317–25.

Slowikowski, S.S. 1993. Cultural performance and sport mascots. *Journal of Sport Issues* 17 (1):23–33.

Spergel, I.A., and S.F. Grossman. 1997. The little village project: A community approach to the gang problem. *Social Work* 42 (5):456–70.

Staurowsky, E.J. 1998. An act of honor or exploitation? The Cleveland Indians' use of the Louis Francis Sockalexis story. *Sociology of Sport Journal* 15 (4):299–316.

Tatz, C. 1995. *Obstacle Race: Aborigines in Sport*. Sydney: University New South Wales Press.

Tatz, C., and D. Adair. 2009. Darkness and a little light: 'Race' and sport in Australia. *Australian Aboriginal Studies* 2:1–14.

Teit, J. 1909. *The Shuswap: The Jesup North Pacific Expedition*. Vol. 2. New York: American Museum of Natural History.

Tindall, B. 1995. Beyond fun and games: Emerging roles of public recreation. *Parks and Recreation* 30 (3):86–93.

Van Maanen, J., ed. 1983. *Qualitative Methodology*. Beverly Hills: Sage Publications.

Venn, C., and M. Featherstone. 2006. Modernity. *Theory, Culture & Society* 23 (2–3):457–65.

Vickers, S. 1998. *Native American Identities: From Stereotype to Archetype in Art and Literature*. Albuquerque: University of New Mexico Press.

Wagg, S., ed. 2005. *Cricket and National Identity in the Postcolonial Age: Following On*. London: Routledge.

Wallerstein, I. 1974a. *The Modern World-System I: Capitalist Agriculture and the Origins of the European World-Economy in the Sixteenth Century*. Vol. 1. New York: Academic Press.

———. 1974b. *The Modern World-System II: Mercantilism and the Consolidation of the European World-Economy, 1600–1750*. Vol. 2. New York: Academic Press.

Weaver, H. 2002. Perspectives on wellness: Journeys on the Red Road. *Journal of Sociology and Social Welfare* 29 (1):5–15.

Weiss, R.P. 1994. *Learning from Strangers: The Art and Method of Qualitative Interview Studies*. New York: The Free Press.

Whitehead, M. 1981. *The Cariboo Mission: A History of the Oblates*. Victoria, BC: Sono Nis Press.

Whitson, D. 1984. Sport and hegemony: On the construction of the dominant culture. *Sociology of Sport Journal* 1 (1):64–78.

Williams, P. 1999. Regina's youth strategy: A community initiative. *Recreation Saskatchewan* 26 (9):4.

Wilson, S., and M. Lipsey. 2000. Wilderness challenge programs for delinquent youth: A meta-analysis of outcome evaluations. *Evaluation and Program Planning* 23 (1):1–12.

York, G. 1989. *The Dispossessed: Life and Death in Native Canada*. Toronto: Lester and Orpen Dennys.

Index

African American double consciousness, 132–3
Afzal-Khan, Fawzia, 22
alcohol use: at Esketemc First Nation, 28–9, 32–5, 38; at tournaments, 76, 89, 114, 121–2, 127–8; treatment for alcohol abuse, 36–7
Alkali Lake (Esket), British Columbia, 28, 30. See also Esketemc First Nation
Alkali Lake Braves Tournament, 9, 34
American Indian Integration of Baseball, The (Powers-Beck), 25
Arguedas, Jose Maria, 131
Australia, indigenous sports, 36

baseball, 25
Beyond a Boundary (James), 3–4, 5
Bhabha, Homi, 19, 147
Birrell, Susan, 23
Bloom, John, 25–6
Bopp, Michael and Judie, 29, 33
border thinking, 20–7, 132–3; as alternative knowledge formation, 20–1; and assimilation, 144; border gnoseology, 20, 131, 151; coloniality and colonialism, 12, 132, 144; double consciousness, 129, 131–5, 142, 147; and indigenous epistemologies, 133–4; in literature and visual arts, 20–2; as local transformation of global practices, 21, 53, 106–7, 128, 148; overview of, 16, 20–7, 132–3; and signification, 19–20, 26–7, 53, 57, 147, 150; in sport, 22–3. See also knowledge and ways of knowing; modernity and coloniality
border thinking and hockey, 130–44; and competitiveness, 141–3; double consciousness, 142, 147; and gnoseology, 131; and modernity, 134–5; overview of, 26–7, 53, 141–4, 150–1; pluriversality of, 135–8, 148; toughness of players, 138–41
Bourdieu, Pierre, 47–8
Brandon, Manitoba, 61–2, 114–15. See also Winter Tribal Days
Brathwaite, Edward Kamau, 20–1
Burstyn, Varda, 36

Cape Breton University, 133
Chelsea, Phyllis, 39, 58
Chingee, Harley, 76–9, 83
Chipewyan epistemology, 134
Civilizational Process, The (Ribeiro),
  15
coaches, hockey, 70, 104, 106
Collings, Peter, 137
coloniality. *See* modernity and
  coloniality
Colonizer and the Colonized, The
  (Memmi), 133
Condon, Richard, 137
coureurs des bois, 111
cricket, 3, 4–5, 23, 51
Culture and Imperialism (Said), 3–4,
  6, 15

Dakota Ojibway Tribal Council,
  62, 64
Deloria, Vine, 18
Discipline and Punish (Foucault),
  47–8, 49, 51
Dispossessed, The (York), 28–9, 38
Dog Creek (Place), 56–7
double consciousness, 129, 131–5,
  142, 147
Du Bois, W.E.B., 131–3
Durieu missionary system, 31–2
Dussel, Enrique, 17

Ekhom-Friedman, Kajasa, 21
Elders: attendance at tournaments,
  88, 115; cultural transmission
  by, 39; grandmothers, 138; as
  hockey fans, 45, 126; honouring
  of, 103; and indigenous ways
  of knowing, 133; and intergenerational contact, 37, 44; pre-
  hockey sweat lodges, 39–44; on
  racism and self-image, 126–7,
  129, 138; as spiritual presences,
  53–5; on toughness, 138, 140; on
  value of tournaments, 115
epistemology. *See* knowledge and
  ways of knowing
equipment, hockey: in recreational
  hockey, 7, 45, 51–2, 139–40;
  in tournaments, 70, 105, 107,
  139–40
Esket (Alkali Lake), British Columbia, 28–30. *See also* Esketemc
  First Nation
Esketemc First Nation: alcohol
  and substance abuse, 28–9,
  32–5, 38; Chief's statements
  on sport, 28, 50–1, 53, 98, 143;
  Elders, 37, 39–44, 45; film on,
  29, 32, 33, 39, 58; healing after
  suicide, 53–5, 57–8; healing by
  culture and sport, 33–4, 37, 55,
  142–3; history of, 28–33, 39,
  56–8; isolation of reserve, 10–11,
  30, 34–5; overview of research,
  10–11; residential school im-
  pacts, 33, 39, 50, 55, 57; sweat
  lodges, 39–44, 55, 57–8; tournament, 9, 34
Esketemc First Nation and
  hockey: arenas, 10–11, 34–5,
  44–5; body-object complex,
  51–2; and border thinking, 53,
  137; equipment and uniforms,
  45, 51–2, 139–40; famous team,
  56–8; as intergenerational
  event, 37, 52–4; recreational
  games, 44–6, 51–3, 58; youth
  hockey initiative, 29, 34–8, 46,
  52–3

Featherstone, Mike, 17
females. *See* women

First Nation Winter Celebration, Brandon, Manitoba, 62, 64. *See also* Winter Tribal Days

First Nations hockey. *See* hockey and First Nations peoples

First Nations reserves, 8n1, 126. *See also* Esketemc First Nation; Sandy Lake First Nation

First Nations spirituality. *See* spirituality, First Nations

First Nations sports. *See* sports and First Nations peoples

First Nations University of Canada, 64

Fisher, Donald, 26

Forsyth, Janice, 24–5

Fort Chipewyan, Alberta, 134

Foucault, Michel: on body as subject of control, 47–8, 49, 51; body-object complex, 13, 49–52; on local knowledges, 19, 21; panopticon, 48–9; on sport, 13

Friedman, Jonathan, 21

Furniss, Elizabeth, 31–2

gender power constructs, 138. *See also* women

gnosis. *See* border thinking

goaltender clinics for youth, 8, 34

goaltender protection, 105

Grant, George, 18–19

Gray, Dennis, 36

Gruneau, Richard, 22–3, 47

Habermas, Jürgen, 17–18, 19

Heine, Mike, 24–5

hockey and Euro-Canadian peoples: and alcohol, 120–1; and masculine constructs of power, 138; and national and cultural identity, 4; and sports-manship, 116–17, 142; and style of play, 12–13, 51–2, 96–7, 105, 142; tournaments, 114, 119–21; violence, 96–7, 118–20

hockey and First Nations peoples: and assimilation, 49–50; body-object complex (Foucault), 13, 49–52; as border thinking, 128–9; as community expression, 13, 26–7, 142–3; and Euro-Canadian hockey, 12–13, 96–7, 116–21, 138, 142; goaltender protection, 105; heroes, 90–2, 148–50; as local cultural practice, 59, 106, 148; and national and cultural identities, 4, 6, 24, 26–7, 97–8; and NHL players, 90–8, 149–50; passion for, 5, 26, 59, 98, 108, 150; process vs. outcome, 52, 139, 142–3; professional hockey's impact on, 84–5, 105–7. *See also* border thinking and hockey; recreational hockey; sports and First Nations peoples; tournaments

hockey and First Nations style of play: bodychecking, 69, 77; body-object complex (Foucault), 13, 49–52; comparison with Euro-Canadian hockey, 51–2, 96–7, 142; competitiveness, 84, 96–8, 141–3; dangle, 45; domination and posturing, 117, 136–7; goaltenders, 105; meaning and local hockey, 106–7; overtime format, 71–2; in pick-up hockey, 7; sensory awareness, 7; 'when it's over, it's over,' 96–7. *See also* border thinking and hockey

Holman, Nunavut, 137

Honour of All, The (film), 29, 32, 33, 39, 58

humour: private jokes, 82–3; and racial tensions, 81, 127; and self-deprecation, 76, 80, 81; and stereotypes, 79–80; storytelling at tournaments, 78–83, 122; and violence, 80–1, 86

Indian Act, 31–2
Indigenous and Popular Thinking in América (Kusch), 130
Inuit recreation, 137
Invention of Africa, The (Mudimbe), 20
Invention of the Americas, The (Dussel), 17

James, C.L.R., 3–5, 23, 50
Jones, Don: on elite hockey, 87; hockey career of, 7, 61, 66, 68–9, 78; on hockey pride, 119; on hockey tournaments, 80, 85, 119; on hockey violence, 117–18; on social events at hockey tournaments, 121–2; as story-teller, 78–9, 81, 122; support for research project, 7–8, 9, 61, 78

Kainai First Nation, Alberta, 88, 110–11
Keewatin, Ontario, 68
Kenequanash, Margaret, 101–2
Kenora, Ontario, 68. *See also* North American First Nations Winter-fest Tournament of Champions
knowledge and ways of knowing: and border thinking, 133–4, 144; 'bush consciousness,' 134; and double consciousness, 133–4; and feminine constructs of

power, 138; Foucault on local knowledges, 19; Habermas on, 17–18; integration of Western and indigenous, 133–4; Inuit hockey and, 137; modernity and privileging of reason and tech-nology, 17–20, 130; Mudimbe on, 20; mythical worldviews, 18; pluriversality of sports, 143, 148; research, modernity and, 151. *See also* border thinking; Elders
Kusch, Rodolfo, 130

lacrosse, 6, 26, 50, 97–8, 111
Lane, Phil, 29
Lethbridge Hurricanes, Alberta, 88
Lightning, Albert, 39, 58
Local Histories/Global Designs (Mignolo), 16
Long, Norman, 21–2
Lumber Kings hockey team, Prince George, British Colum-bia, 78–83, 115–16
Lumber Kings tournament. *See* Prince George Lumber Kings Annual All-Native Hockey Tournament

Making of High Performance Athletes (Shogan), 48
Marshall, Albert, 133
medicine wheel, 34, 37, 44
Memmi, Albert, 133
Men at Play (Robidoux), 6
Menchú, Rigoberta, 131
Mignolo, Walter: border think-ing, 16, 20–1, 128, 131–3, 144; on Brathwaite, 20–1; colonial semiosis, 19, 26–7; coloniality vs. colonialism, 12, 132; double

consciousness, 131; gnosis and gnoseology, 20–1, 131; local transformation of global practices, 128, 142, 144; modern and indigenous knowledge, 130; pluritopic hermeneutics, 144; pluriversality, 134–5. *See also* border thinking; modernity and coloniality

Mi'kmaq Nation, 133

missionaries, 31–2, 57–8

Moccasin Game, 62

modernity and coloniality: and border thinking, 132–3, 147; colonial semiosis, 19, 26–7; coloniality vs. colonialism, 12, 132; cultural interrelatedness and, 15–17; and double consciousness, 129, 131–5, 142, 147; empire expansionism, 17–18; local transformation of global practices, 128; overview of, 16, 132–3, 150; and privileging of progress, reason, and technology, 17–20, 59, 130; and sport, 134–5. *See also* border thinking

Mongia, Padmani, 22

Mudimbe, Valentin, 20

National Hockey League: Aboriginal fans, 5, 26, 90; Aboriginal players, 87–8, 90–2, 148–50

North American First Nations Winterfest Tournament of Champions, Kenora, Ontario, 68–75; community gathering at, 73, 86–7, 118; monetary incentives for players, 68, 70, 75; overtime format, 71–2; overview of, 68–70; prestige and honour, 70, 75; skill level discrepancies, 69, 70, 73–4, 86; violence, 73–4, 75, 86, 118; youth development, 74–5

North American Indigenous Games, 24

North Battleford, Saskatchewan, 113

Northern First Nations Hockey Tournament, Sioux Lookout, Ontario, 98–108; after-tournament events, 123; community gathering at, 99, 107–9, 114; discriminatory accommodation policies, 115; equipment and uniforms, 105, 107; honouring Elders, 103; host town, 99, 115, 123–4; as intergenerational event, 102; monetary incentives for players, 99, 103; overview of, 98–100, 114; passion for hockey, 108; prestige and honour, 103, 107–9, 139; professional hockey's impact on, 105–7; as recreational tournament, 99–100; research relationships, 100–1; skill level discrepancies, 102, 107–8; toughness of players, 103–5, 139; tournament organization, 101–2

Odjick, Gino, 87–8, 90–6

Oka crisis, 79

Olympic Games, 22

Orientalism (Said), 15

Paraschak, Victoria, 24–5, 147

Perrot, Nicolas, 111

Place, Hilary, 56–7

Potskin, Corey, 83

Powers-Beck, Jeffrey, 25

Pratt, Mary Louise, 17, 19
Prince, Joe, 82–3
Prince George, British Columbia, 76, 122–3
Prince George Lumber Kings Annual All-Native Hockey Tournament, 75–98; brawls and violence, 77, 81, 85–6, 118–19; community gathering at, 88; community teams and rivalries, 77, 84–7, 118–19; divisions, 76, 77, 83–5, 87–9; humorous events, 76, 77, 80–3, 86, 89; monetary incentives for players, 82, 87; and NHL players, 90–8; overview of, 75–7; skill discrepancies, 83–5; storytelling at, 77–83; toughness of players, 91–3, 138; tournament organizer, 76–9, 83; women's hockey, 76, 77

Quijano, Anibal, 15, 16, 132

race and racism: 'arrival' as integration, 3–5; chronic racial tensions, 81, 109, 123–8; critical race theory and sports, 23–4; cultural resistance and sports, 23–7, 50–1; double consciousness, 129, 132–3; and humour, 81, 127; and self-image, 126–7, 129, 138; and stereotypes, 79–80, 110–12, 114, 116, 148; and storytelling, 80–1, 122; and violence, 123–4, 128
recreational hockey: as alcohol-free events, 38; equipment, 139–40; overview of, 10–11; pick-up games, 7, 135–7, 140;

researcher's participation in, 8–9, 135–7, 142–3. *See also* Esketemc First Nation and hockey; Sandy Lake First Nation
referees, 78–9, 103–4, 142
Report of the Royal Commission on Aboriginal Peoples, 36
research project (Robidoux), 6–14; data collection and analysis, 9–12, 83; existing studies, 141–2; genesis of, 6–7; participants in, 146–7; points of tension/conflict (defamiliarization), 51, 83, 93, 135–7, 146; recreational hockey, 10–11; researcher's background, 6–7, 13–14; researcher's participation in, 6–8, 10–11, 122, 145–7; support from Don Jones for, 7–8, 9, 61, 78; theoretical framework, 12–14; tournament hockey, 9–10, 59, 61, 116–17; women's hockey, 64n4. *See also* Jones, Don; Robidoux, Michael
reserves, First Nations, 8n1, 126. *See also* Esketemc First Nation; Sandy Lake First Nation
residential schools, 25–6, 33, 50, 57
Ribeiro, Darcy, 15
Robidoux, Michael: as hockey player and instructor, 8, 34, 100, 119–21; on personal impact of project, 150–1; previous research on hockey, 6, 114; sweat lodge experience, 39–44. *See also* research project (Robidoux)

Saggers, Sherry, 36
Said, Edward, 3–4, 6, 15, 22
Sandy Bay First Nation, Manitoba, 66–7

Sandy Lake First Nation, Ontario: overview of research, 10–11; pick-up hockey, 135–7, 140–1; researcher's relationship with, 100, 145

Schultz, Dave, 94

Scollon, Ronald, and Suzanne B.K. Scollon, 133–4

Secwepmc Nation. *See* Esketemc First Nation

Shogan, Debra, 48

Shuswap peoples, 30–1, 44

Sioux Lookout, Ontario, 99, 115, 123–4. *See also* Northern First Nations Hockey Tournament

Sioux Valley Dakota First Nation, 62, 64, 67

Souls of Black Folk, The (Du Bois), 132

spirituality, First Nations: and alcohol abuse treatment, 36–7; and ancestors, 53–5; and hockey, 28, 44, 143, 148; medicine wheel, 34, 37, 44; sweat lodges, 39–44, 55, 57–8

sports and First Nations peoples: and assimilation, 3–4, 24–6, 49–50; comparison with Euro-Canadian hockey, 116–17, 138, 142; competitiveness, 84, 96–8, 141–3; control and discipline, 13, 35–6, 46–9, 134–5; and critical race theory, 23–4; and critical sports studies, 48, 141–2; and cultural resistance, 23–7, 50–1; and indigenous identities, 24–7, 96–8; pluriversality of, 134–7, 143, 148; team logo imagery, 112; toughness of hockey players, 91–6, 103–5, 138–41; 'when it's over, it's over' in hockey, 96–7. *See also* border thinking and hockey; hockey and First Nations peoples; lacrosse; violence

stereotypes. *See* race and racism

storytelling: healing after suicide, 53–5, 57–8; as individual or collective performances, 78, 80; at tournaments, 77–83, 122

Sudbury, Ontario, 113

sweat lodges, 39–44, 55, 57–8

Swift Lake, Ontario, 65–6

Theory of Communicative Action, The (Habermas), 17–18, 19

To Show What an Indian Can Do (Bloom), 25–6

Tootoo, Jordin, 90

tournaments: and alcohol use, 76, 89, 114, 121–2, 127–8; body-contact events, 69, 73; coaches, 70, 104, 106; community gatherings at, 86–8, 97–9, 107–9, 114, 119, 127; comparison with Euro-Canadian tournaments, 114, 119–21; competitiveness, 84, 96–8, 141–3; diversity of, 108; future directions, 87; incentives for host towns, 113–14; meaning to fans, 108, 115–16; overview of, 9–10, 59–61, 108–9; professional hockey's impact on, 84–5, 105–7; violence and public disorder at, 74, 113, 119, 122, 124, 127–8. *See also* race and racism; violence

tournaments, community-based, 98–108; as alcohol-free events, 76, 121; community gathering

at, 99, 107–9, 119; competitiveness, 96–8; equipment and
uniforms, 105, 107, 139–40;
monetary incentives for players,
98, 99, 103; overview of, 60–1,
98; prestige and honour, 107–9,
119; professional hockey's
impact on, 105–7; skill level
discrepancies, 98; toughness of
players, 103–5. *See also* Northern
First Nations Hockey Tournament, Sioux Lookout
tournaments, high performance,
61–98; as alcohol-free events,
76, 121; bodychecking, 69, 77;
community gathering at, 97–8,
119; competitiveness, 84, 96–8;
equipment and uniforms,
139–40; monetary incentives for
players, 64–6, 68, 75, 87, 108–9;
overview of, 60–1; prestige and
honour, 65–7, 108–9, 119; professional hockey's impact on,
84–5; referees, 78–9; skill level
discrepancies, 69, 84–5; storytelling, 77–83; 'when it's over,
it's over,' 96–7. *See also* North
American First Nations Winter-
fest Tournament of Champions;
Prince George Lumber Kings
Annual All-Native Hockey
Tournament; Winter Tribal Days

Van Maanen, John, 11
Venn, Couze, 17
Vickers, Scott B., 21
violence, 116–27; brawls at tournaments, 73–4, 79, 81–2, 118–19;
community rivalries at tournaments, 77, 85–7; comparison
with Euro-Canadian hockey,
92, 96–7, 118–19; fan participation, 85–6, 118–19; and honour,
94–6; and humour, 80–1, 86;
incidents in communities, 119,
122–4, 127–8; incidents on ice,
116–19, 127–8; Inuit 'bothering,'
137; posturing by players, 117;
and racial tensions, 81, 123–8;
stereotypes of, 110–12, 114,
116, 148; and storytelling, 122;
toughness of players, 103–5,
138–41. *See also* alcohol use

Wallerstein, Immanuel, 15–16
Wamsley, Kevin, 24
Weaver, Hillary, 37
Whitehead, Margaret, 31
Whitson, David, 49
Williams Lake, British Columbia,
11, 30, 44
Winnipeg, Manitoba, recreation
programming, 25
Winter Tribal Days, Brandon,
Manitoba, 61–7; festival events,
62–3; finances, 64–5, 67; hockey
divisions, 63–4; host town,
61–2, 114–15; as intergenerational event, 62–4, 67; monetary
incentives, 63, 64–5; overtime
format, 71; overview of, 61–2,
67; prestige and honour, 65–7
women: hockey players, 11, 64,
76, 77; power of grandmothers,
138; and sobriety movement at
Esketemc, 39; at sweat lodges,
42; tournament organizers,
101–2

York, Geoffrey, 28–9, 38

ERIC'S DISCOVERY

CHOICE BOOKS
The Best In Family Reading
P. O. Box 503
Goshen, IN 46526
"We Welcome Your Response"

ERIC'S DISCOVERY

Dorothy Hamilton

Illustrated by
Betty Wind

HERALD PRESS
Scottdale, Pennsylvania
Kitchener, Ontario
1979

Library of Congress Cataloging in Publication Data
Hamilton, Dorothy, 1906-
  Eric's discovery.

  SUMMARY: After witnessing the vandalizing of a
church, a young boy doesn't know if he should tell
anyone what and whom he saw.
  [1. Vandalism—Fiction] I. Wind, Betty.
II. Title.
PZ7.H18136Er [Fic]   79-18537
ISBN 0-8361-1902-9
ISBN 0-8361-1903-7 pbk.

ERIC'S DISCOVERY
Copyright © 1979 by Herald Press, Scottdale, Pa. 15683
    Published simultaneously in Canada by Herald Press,
    Kitchener, Ont. N2G 4M5
Library of Congress Catalog Card Number: 79-18537
International Standard Book Numbers:
    0-8361-1902-9 (hardcover)
    0-8361-1903-7 (softcover)
Printed in the United States of America
Design: Alice B. Shetler

15 14 13 12 11 10 9 8 7 6 5 4 3 2 1